March 1983

WATER PROBLEMS IN OIL PRODUCTION

An Operator's Manual

Water Problems in Oil Production

An Operator's Manual

Second Edition

L. C. CASE, M. A.

PennWell Books
PennWell Publishing Company
Tulsa, Oklahoma

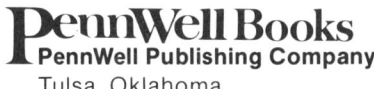

© Copyright, 1970
The PennWell Publishing Company

1421 South Sheridan
Tulsa, OK 74101

ALL RIGHTS RESERVED
This book or any part thereof may
not be reproduced in any form without
permission of the publisher

Library of Congress Catalog Card Number: 75-118940
International Standard Book Number 87814-001-8
Printed in U.S.A.

Second Edition, 1977

4 5 6 7 8 • 85 84 83 82 81

The oil industry has given me a comfortable living, filled with many challenges, and a host of friends. For these, I am deeply grateful. It follows that this book is the final result of a long-term effort to leave something of practical value. I hope that the time and care spent in preparation of this operator's manual will repay, in some small measure, the debt which has accumulated over a period of forty-five years.

L. C. Case

Table of Contents

	Foreword	ix
	Preface	x
1	Introductory Remarks, Scope, and Limitations of Water Injection Problems	1
2	Waterflood Practice, General Discussion, Common Problems, and Certain Recommendations for Initial Consideration	4
3	Water Chemistry—the Compounds Commonly in Solution in Natural Waters	7
4	Solid Deposits—Scale Formation	22
5	Corrosion Causes, Prevention, and Treatment	39
6	Plugging or Fouling Deposits	51
7	Filtration	56
8	Identification of Common Problems Due to Water and Corrective Measures	60
9	Some Specifications for Injection Water	84
10	How to Avoid Pollution and Combat Unjust Claims	96
11	Bimetallic or Electrical Gadgets, Radioactive Mechanisms, and other Mystic Devices for Preventing Corrosion, Scale, and Associated Problems	106
12	Criteria for Choosing Qualified Services Relating to Water Problems	115
13	Oil-In-Water Emulsions, Causes, and Treatment	123

TABLES

1.	Positive and Negative Radicles Present in all Natural Waters, with Valences and Reaction Coefficients	8
2.	Fresh Waters	11

vii

TABLE OF CONTENTS

3. Brackish Waters and Dilute Brines — 13
4. Brines Produced with Oil — 15
5. Derivation of a Balanced Water Analysis from the Essential Cations and Anions — 21
6. Guide to Field Identification of Scales and Probable Causes — 23

CHARTS

1. Gypsum Solubility Curve — 27
2. Comparison of Membrane Filter Tests, at 20 psi, Two Injection Wells in Different Waterfloods — 90
3. Schematic Water Treating System — 131
4. Flotation Systems — 134
5. Air Flotation System, Fully Pressurized Aeration — 135
6. Air Flotation Unit, Recycle Water Aeration — 137
7. Induced Air Froth Flotation Unit — 138

PLATES

1. Scale Build-up—Injection Lines — 41
2. Graphitic Corrosion — 42
3. Sweet-oil (organic acid) corrosion — 43
4. Carbon dioxide corrosion — 44

Appendix

Well Leaks as Indicated by Water Analysis — 142
Check List for Trouble Finding at Water Floods — 144
Guide for Selection of Metals & Alloys for "Sour" Salt Water Service — 147
Equivalents for Determining Hypothetical Combinations, in the Order in Which They React — 149
Calcium Carbonate Weight Factors — 151
Table of Conversion Factors and Equivalents — 152
Specific Gravity vs Total Solids — 153
An Editorial, *Corrosion,* July, 1960 (Concerning the magic, water-treating gadgets) — 154
API Form 45-1: API Water Analysis Report Form — 157
Generalized Design for Split Water Injection System — 158

Index — 159

viii

Foreword

This book is an attempt to assemble and correlate a number of easily-recognized, fundamental causes and their effects in logical sequence, such that certain observations may lead unerringly to practical solutions of common waterflood problems. Preparative discussion of basic chemical relationships, preceding Chapter 8, may seem elementary and repetitious to some, or lacking in sufficient detail to others. The first would represent the lesser evil. A possible correction to omission of more complete description and illustrations is available in the few selected references at the end of each chapter.

In any event, the principles set forth, prior to Chapter 8, must be understood and employed in any successful application of the practical solutions given in Chapter 8. These basic principles have not failed to identify operating difficulties and their causes at a great many water injection plants. Nevertheless, invention is neither indicated nor implied. Only the manner of presenting this material is different. If it clearly reflects the author's *modus operandi*, then the intended purpose, and hopefully a useful one, has been served.

It will be noted that details for making field tests and various laboratory analyses are not included in this book. These have been treated adequately in several, readily available publications. Nevertheless, explanation and illustration of troubles and their causes are believed to be comprehensive, to the extent that selection of the few necessary tests will be indicated for any given water problem. Logically then, it should follow that familiarity with this book will enable a field engineer to correctly assess the conditions existing at any waterflood or disposal project and to use only those remedial methods which are proved for known purposes.

Preface

I am indebted to many people of several oil companies, service companies and laboratories, for much of the data related to location of water troubles and their alleviation. Although most of the material for this book was collected during twelve years of consulting work, appreciable involvement with water troubles took place before 1930. The challenge of these problems led quite naturally to continued and systematic accumulation of library material and data concerning oil field water problems and their solutions.

Seven years of usage of the first edition have shown successful application of the manual at many waterfloods and disposal operations. However, this revised edition contains a much-needed additional chapter on emulsions in waste oil field waters. The writer is especially grateful to Dr. R. J. Churchill, Tretolite Div. of Petrolite Corp., for necessary suggestions and to Fred W. Jenkins for writing Chapter 13, "Oil-in-Water Emulsions."

L. C. Case
Tulsa, Oklahoma
May 13, 1977

1

Introductory Remarks, Scope and Limitations of Water Injection Problems

The rather all-inclusive title of this book might be more properly applied to a book of more impressive proportions. In the event that the monumental task of assembling the data for such a book can ever be completed, publication should follow within a few years. In the meantime, the need is now for a working manual, to serve as a ready reference in recognition, prevention and remedy of the many problems in oil production that are due, either directly or indirectly, to water.

Although most of these problems occur in waterflood operation, many similar ones, due to the same causes, are encountered in primary production and in salt water disposal to underground formations. Logically, the troubles causing operating expense, due to water, should be least in primary production, appreciably greater in salt water disposal, and greatest in waterflood operation. Under average conditions, this relationship assumes the status of a general rule. For example, "formation water" produced with oil is usually brought to the surface without mixing with other waters or coming into contact with air.

Although scale or corrosion may take place within the well bore, the remedies are usually positive, relatively simple, and economical. When pumping waste brine to an underground formation, good fortune may provide a very permeable zone at

WATER PROBLEMS IN OIL PRODUCTION
An Operator's Manual

shallow depth. Even so, the zone may become plugged due to incompatible waters, injection of excessive silt, trash, dirty oil, or oil emulsion.

The time factor provided by various holding vessels tends to multiply the formation of deposits. In addition, the tanks usually allow ample opportunity for the growth of harmful bacteria. In common waterflood practice, far too many of the evil influences are usually present. Under average conditions, the minimum, or necessary, holding vessels and injection lines provide time for unwanted reactions, and additional tanks increase the effect enormously.

It has been observed during many inspections of water injecting equipment that the magnitude of operating problems is more or less in direct ratio to the number of waters mixed and their standing time before injection. Air leaks are often a contributing factor where systems were designed to be closed but fail to operate as such. One or more examples of very small air leaks, directly causing severe damage, will be given later in some detail.

In summary, the complex conditions present at most waterfloods are conducive to eventual troubles, which vary in nature and degree according to the existing conditions.

From the foregoing it is seen that water provides a medium for chemical reactions that result in operating problems. In order to recognize these problems and to choose preventive or remedial methods, it is necessary to understand water. All the fundamentals for this understanding are set forth in the chapter on water chemistry. Use of this manual should not be attempted without spending sufficient time on these rather simple chemical relationships to learn the components of water solutions and their possible reactions. With this knowledge, the reader will know why deposits form and something as to the limitations of their composition.

Additionally, this prerequisite in chemistry provides a basis for identifying many of the processes of corrosion and their

*Introductory Remarks, Scope, and Limitations
of Water Injection Problems*

prevention or treatment. Last but not least, this background information, together with an assessment of existing conditions, places an operating engineer in a position to challenge and discard all misleading tests and faulty interpretation—which are always available.

The twofold purpose of this book should now be apparent. Full realization of the possibilities when mixing and handling waters should permit planning and design against operating difficulties of costly proportions. Where troubles are unavoidably present, the challenge of surveying the existing conditions and pinpointing the major causes may be met successfully.

2

Waterflood Practice, General Discussion, Common Problems and Certain Recommendations for Initial Consideration

Normally, it is not possible to select an ideal water for supply when planning a given waterflood. Rather, economics dictate that a water be used which is readily available. Such source may consist of shallow wells, streams or impoundments. In such event, the water will almost always contain dissolved oxygen—infamous for causing corrosion in any brine, especially in the sour ones.

Obviously, closed systems and gas seals on tanks are of no benefit when oxygen-containing water is mixed with produced brine prior to injection. In view of the many objections to mixing oxygen-containing fresh water with produced brines, it should be emphasized that split systems are usually found advantageous where no other solution is possible. Open systems, especially where settling ponds and filtration are employed, have proved generally unsatisfactory.

It follows that closed systems are much to be preferred, due to their fewer and relatively simpler operating problems. The term "closed system" should connote total exclusion of air. The main effects of air entry and some simple means of its detection will be considered under the subject of corrosion.

There are numerous areas under waterflood where a choice was initially available as to a source of supply water. For example, where supply wells were completed in the first shallow zone furnishing adequate water volume, drilling a few

Waterflood Practice, General Discussion, Common Problems and Certain Recommendations for Initial Consideration

hundred feet more would have assured an oxygen-free brine which was compatible in all respects with produced brine.

This introduces a subject which has definitely not received deserved attention. While it has been observed for many years that waterfloods handling only heavy salt water have the least operating trouble, the underlying causes have largely escaped explanation and emphasis. At the outset, it may be said that strong brines, free of oxygen and hydrogen sulfide, are essentially non-corrosive—except for rare cases of "sweet oil" corrosion due to organic acids. These heavy brines are not good solvents for the acid gases. Thus, attack by acid gases is mild in the absence of air.

The saline brines do not contain large amounts of bicarbonates, thus scaling is minimum. Finally, it has been shown that corrosive bacteria, which produce H_2S, grow very slowly in brines of over 100,000 mg/l concentration. This is a valid explanation of the harmless amounts of sulfide found in very salty brine systems after several years of operation.

Operating difficulties at waterfloods consist mainly of corrosion, scaling of equipment, and plugging by suspended solids or slime. The variable conditions at waterfloods may cause only one, or perhaps all three conditions to occur simultaneously. It is therefore axiomatic that neighboring waterfloods usually have less resemblance than widely separated oil pools. Nevertheless, the troubles are closely related as to origin.

Corrosion attacks metals, mainly steel, and the products of the corrosion process may add measurably to adhering deposits or entrained suspended matter. Adhering deposits cause localized corrosion in two ways. The deposits, or scale, are both discontinuous and porous. In addition, the thicker, loosely adhering deposits promote the growth of anaerobic, corrosive bacteria under them. Organic slimes, plus the usual amounts of oil emulsion and particulate matter, may cause serious plugging of injection wells when the formation is relatively tight.

WATER PROBLEMS IN OIL PRODUCTION
An Operator's Manual

All of these problems have basic causes. Identification of these causes is a necessary approach to any remedial measures at a troublesome waterflood. Proper selection of tests to establish significant data and proof of the undesirable processes requires acquaintance with the chemical reactions which can, and usually do, take place in the presence of water. Such understanding can best be accomplished by consideration of the fundamentals of water chemistry. Although waters differ widely in characteristics, the unwanted reactions are relatively simple in nature and limited by the few compounds present in natural water solutions.

3

Water Chemistry—the Compounds Commonly in Solution in Natural Waters

The common elements, or radicles, in water constitute a balance of positive and negative ions. These ions combine with one or more other ions or radicles to form salts. Thus sodium sulfate, Na_2SO_4, is an equivalent weight of $Na+$ with an equivalent weight of $SO_4^=$, which illustrates the balance of a positive ion with a negative radicle. Other terms often applied to the elements and radicles are "basic" and "acidic," or the equivalent "cations" and "anions."

Any statement of physical weights of ions or radicles indicates only the chemical composition of a water, but not its character. To reflect the true character of a water, the relative chemical equivalent combining weights must be shown. These equivalents, or reaction capacities, are found by dividing atomic weight by valence. Thus, the relative proportions are shown in view of chemical reaction, or combination. For example, calcium chloride is written $CaCl_2$, since two monovalent Cl ions are required to balance the divalent calcium ion. On the other hand, calcium oxide is written CaO because the divalent calcium and oxygen ions are chemically equivalent. The law of chemical equivalents is clearly shown below.

Element or Radicle	Atomic Weight	Equivalent Weight
Calcium	40.09	$\frac{40.09}{2} = 20.045$

WATER PROBLEMS IN OIL PRODUCTION
An Operator's Manual

Chloride	35.457	$\dfrac{35.457}{1} = 35.457$
Oxygen	16	$\dfrac{16}{2} = 8$

As above illustrated, the ratio in which the positive and negative ions combine is governed by their respective valences. Table 1 lists the more common positive and negative radicles

TABLE 1. Positive and Negative Radicles Present in All Natural Waters, with Valences and Reaction Coefficients.

Positive Radicles	Valence	R.Coef.
Alkali:		
Sodium, Na	1	.0435
Potassium, K	1	.0256
(Also, less commonly lithium, rubidium, caesium and ammonium. The latter, NH_4, is somewhat common in oil field brines).		
Alkaline Earth:		
Calcium, Ca	2	.0499
Magnesium, Mg	2	.0822
Barium, Ba	2	.0146
Strontium, Sr	2	.0228
Metals:		
Aluminum, Al	3	.1107
Iron, Fe	3	.0537
Manganese, Mn	2	.0364
(Also trace amounts of many other metals. Aluminum and iron are generally thought to be present in water, mainly as the colloidal oxides. However, iron is sometimes present as the bicarbonate and has been identified also as being combined with an organic acid radicle. Thus, iron in natural waters usually has a valence of 2, rather than 3 or ferric iron).		

Negative Radicles	Valence	R.Coef.
Strong Acid:		
Chloride, Cl	1	.0282
Sulfate, SO_4	2	.0208
(Also less commonly nitrate, bromide, iodide and thiosulfate. Bromine and iodine are commonly found in oil field brines and the usual small amounts have no relationship to total solids).		
Weak Acid:		
Bicarbonate, HCO_3	1	.0164
Carbonate, CO_3	2	.0333
Sulfide, S	2	.0624
(Also, less commonly Sulfite, SO_3, Phosphate, PO_4, Silicate, SiO_3, and certain organic acid radicles. Silicate is usually reported as silica, SiO_2 and considered to be a colloid. However, in some alkaline fresh waters the silica is combined with alkali and should be calculated accordingly).		

found in water with their valences and "reaction coefficients." These reaction coefficients are used to find the chemical reacting power of the various ions determined in a water analysis. In other words, unit weight of a radicle, or ion,

$$x \frac{\text{Valence}}{\text{Equivalent Wt.}} = \text{its reacting power.}$$

When the unit weight is stated as milligrams per liter, mg/l, the reacting power is the same as "equivalents per liter," "milli-equivalents per liter," frequently abbreviated "E.P.L.," "MEQ." Obviously, calculation of the values is facilitated by multiplying the unit weight by the reciprocal; for example,

mg/l of Ca $\times \frac{1}{20.04}$ (or 0.0499) = E.P.L

Since the analysis must balance, the sum of the positive reacting values is equal to the sum of the negative reacting values. Thus, it is a common practice to lump Sodium (Na) and potassium (K) together by difference, as sodium. Provided that other constituents have been correctly determined, actual separation and measurement of the alkalies is seldom of any significance, potassium being a minor constituent in most of the oilwell brines.

A casual acquaintance with the relationships, as above outlined, allows re-calculation of non-standard water analyses and their reduction to meaningful figures, which in turn may be interpreted or compared with other available water analysis data.

A recent publication, A.P.I.RP 45, Nov., 1965, outlines only one approved method of presenting water analyses; see API form 45–1 in the Appendix. This is the ionic form, as opposed to hypothetical combinations, with the specific gravity of the water to be given at 60°F, and weight: volume concentration stated in milligrams per liter, (mg/l). Parts per million, P.P.M., or ppm, can only be true parts per million if the determined mg/l are divided by specific gravity. Thus, mg/l and ppm are essentially the same for fresh waters.

WATER PROBLEMS IN OIL PRODUCTION
An Operator's Manual

The specific gravity of water has many uses, an outstanding one being a check on the accuracy of a given analysis. As an example, if an analysis stated specific gravity to be 1.100 and total solds to be in the order of 70,000 mg/l, something is obviously in error. This can happen when an analyst uses a measuring pipette one-half the size he thought he was using. Tabulation of approximate total solids vs. sp.gr. is given in the appendix. It should be noted that sp.gr. is significant to the third place only. Determinations to the fourth decimal require extreme care, thus figures given to fourth place should be regarded usually as window dressing.

In total disregard of usual and approved practice, we see numerous water analyses said to be in ppm, grains per gallon or other units. Even worse, some analysts state everything in a water analysis in terms of calcium carbonate, $CaCO_3$. In order to find if these analyses are of any value, it is necessary to reduce them to ionic form. Thereafter, if sufficient tests are stated, the analysis may be checked for equivalence and compared or interpreted.

For example, when calcium and magnesium are stated as $CaCO_3$, there is no need for confusion. It is merely necessary to remember that $CaCO_3 \times \dfrac{Ca}{CaCO_3}$ (or 0.4004) = Ca. Similarly, Mg (as $CaCO_3 \times \dfrac{Mg}{CaCO_3}$ (or 0.243) = Mg. Use atomic and molecular weights, available in any chemical handbook. These and many similar relationships are given in the table of conversion factors, in the appendix, for the purpose of reducing otherwise meaningless figures of water analyses to a common basis, of possible significance and value.

A so-called "complete" water analysis, stated in the ionic form, usually gives a close approximation of total solids. However, the combination of ions to form certain soluble salts is not known unless the analysis is quite simple, with a few ions

Water Chemistry—the Compounds Commonly in Solution in Natural Waters

dominant. It follows that hypothetical combinations may sometimes be calculated to illustrate the outstanding characteristics of a given water.

"Standard Methods for the Examination of Water and Sewage," by Am. Pub. Health Assoc. & Am. Waterworks Assoc., sets forth the approved method and order for calculating hypothetical combinations of the radicles in a water analysis. The method is often useful when illustrating the source of scale-forming compounds, amounts of solids thrown down when mixing incompatible waters, etc. The hypothetical combinations are stated in the tables of water analyses, Tables 2, 3 and 4, as additional criteria in the character of the waters.

TABLE 2. Fresh Waters

		Milligrams per Liter (mg/l)				
Analysis No.		1	2	3	4	5
Sample Source		Well, 300 ft Stephens Co., Oklahoma	Well, 80 ft Fox Field Oklahoma	Well, 150 ft Osage Co., Oklahoma	Well, 18 ft Osage Co., Oklahoma	Alluvium Well, Stonewall Co., Texas
Milligrams per liter	Na	51	877	111	115	647
	Ca	101	5	9	136	586
	Mg	52	4	3	109	83
	SO_4	230	282	32	150	1,852
	Cl	21	485	101	290	750
	HCO_3	378	964	125	588	276
	CO_3	nil	102	nil	nil	nil
Total Solids		833	2,719	381	1,388	4,194
Total Hardness*, in grains/gal & (mg/l)—		27.7(473.7)	1.7(28.9)	2.1(35.7)	47.2(806.7)	105.5(1,806)

Definition of Water Character (Palmer Values) in %					
Primary Salinity	19.54	50.42	63.20	24.04	43.84
Secondary Salinity	26.86	0.00	0.00	10.52	49.10
Primary Alkalinity	0.00	48.08	24.24	0.00	0.00
Secondary Alkalinity	53.60	1.50	12.56	65.44	7.06
	100.00%	100.00%	100.00%	100.00%	100.00%

WATER PROBLEMS IN OIL PRODUCTION
An Operator's Manual

TABLE 2. (Cont.)

Hypothetical Combinations, A.P.H.A. Method of Calculation

Ca(HCO$_3$)$_2$	408	20	36	550	367
Mg(HCO$_3$)$_2$	85	24	18	192	—
NaHCO$_3$	—	1,280	114	—	—
CaCO$_3$	—	—	—	—	—
MgCO$_3$	—	—	—	—	—
Na$_2$CO$_3$	—	180	—	—	—
CaSO$_4$	—	—	—	—	1,683
MgSO$_4$	187	—	—	188	410
Na$_2$SO$_4$	119	416	47	—	496
CaCl$_2$	—	—	—	—	—
MgCl$_2$	—	—	—	152	—
NaCl	34	799	166	291	1,238
Total	833	2,719	381	1,388	4,194

* Total hardness is usually given in grains per gallon. This is followed above by the total hardness in mg/l. This total hardness is always stated in terms of CaCO$_3$, obtained by test, or calculated as follows:

$$\text{Total Hardness, grains per gal. as CaCO}_3 = \frac{\text{mg/l Ca} \times 2.50 + \text{mg/l Mg} \times 4.115}{17.1}$$

Total hardness is usually significant on fresh waters, while the specific gravity is not. For this reason, the hardness is stated instead of the sp.gr.

A somewhat looser characterization of water analyses, although subject to less actual error, is provided by the "Palmer Values" (reference at the end of this chapter). The Palmer values merely equate the alkalies, Na & K, to strong acids, Cl & SO$_4$, remaining strong acids to alkaline earths, Ca & Mg, or remaining alkalies to weak acids, CO$_3$ & HCO$_3$, and, finally, alkaline earths to weak acids to complete the picture, as follows.

Primary Salinity: Alkalies + strong acids, essentially NaCl, Na$_2$SO$_4$.

Secondary Salinity: Alkaline Earths + strong acids, CaCl$_2$, MgCl$_2$, CaSO$_4$, MgSO$_4$

Primary Alkalinity: Alkalies + weak acids, Na$_2$CO$_3$, NaHCO$_3$.

Secondary Alkalinity: Alkaline earths + weak acids, CaCO$_3$, Ca(HCO$_3$)$_2$, MgCO$_3$, Mg(HCO$_3$)$_2$

Water Chemistry—the Compounds Commonly in Solution in Natural Waters

TABLE 3. Brackish Waters and Dilute Brines

Milligrams per liter (mg/l)

Analysis No.		6	7	8	9	10	11
Sample Source		Well, 1560 ft Pontotoc Co., Okla.	Well, 1250 ft Seminole Co., Okla.	Well, 1452 ft Garvin Co., Okla.	Well, 610 ft Oklahoma Co., Okla.	Alluvium Well, 45 ft Stonewall Co., Tex.	Average Sea Water
Milligrams per liter:	Na	2,114	2,414	5,277	5,867	9,080	10,964*
	Ca	17	519	306	538	1,258	420
	Mg	18	74	89	122	338	1,300
	SO_4	20	4,579	0	8,400	2,900	2,700
	Cl	2,630	1,380	8,370	4,040	14,910	19,350
	HCO_3	1,200	170	977	204	274	0
	CO_3	nil	nil	nil	nil	nil	70
Total Solids		5,999	9,136	15,019	19,171	28,760	34,804
Other Constituents:							
H_2S—		Yes	No	No	No	No	No
Barium—		No	No	36 mg/l	No	No	No
Sp.Gr. at 60°F—		1.007	1.008	1.012	1.020	1.022	1.025

Definition of Water Character (Palmer Values) in %

	6	7	8	9	10	11
Primary Salinity	79.12	76.64	91.04	87.36	81.34	78.84
Secondary Salinity	0.00	21.34	2.60	11.50	17.74	21.12
Primary Alkalinity	18.42	0.00	0.00	0.00	0.00	0.00
Secondary Alkalinity	2.46	2.02	6.36	1.14	0.92	0.04
	100.00%	100.00%	100.00%	100.00%	100.00%	100.00%

Hypothetical Combination, A.P.H.A. Method of Calculation, mg/l

	6	7	8	9	10	11
$Ca(HCO_3)_2$	69	226	1,239	271	364	—
$Mg(HCO_3)_2$	108	—	55	—	—	—
$NaHCO_3$	1,457	—	—	—	—	—
$CaCO_3$	—	—	—	—	—	115
$MgCO_3$	—	—	—	—	—	—
Na_2CO_3	—	—	—	—	—	—
$CaSO_4$	—	1,575	—	1,602	3,970	1,272
$MgSO_4$	—	366	—	603	123	2,257
Na_2SO_4	30	4,694	—	10,032	—	—

WATER PROBLEMS IN OIL PRODUCTION
An Operator's Manual

TABLE 3. (Cont.)

CaCl$_2$	—	—	—	—	—	—
MgCl$_2$	—	—	312	—	1,226	3,330
NaCl	4,335	2,275	13,413	6,663	23,077	27,860
Total	5,999	9,136	15,019	19,171	28,760	34,804

* Actually, Ocean water has an average of 390 mg/l of potassium. As with the other analyses, the potassium is calculated by difference as sodium. Separation of the alkalies is ordinarily of no value, thus the calculation by difference is widely used, see A.P.I. RP 45 "Recommended Practice for Analysis of Oil Field Waters," Nov., 1965.

It will be seen that the Palmer values place ions or radicles of similar strength or affinity together, thus avoiding the possible error of stating a great many specific compounds. Since the Palmer values are given in %, the total solids are not indicated. These values often serve as an easier illustration of water character than hypothetical combinations. An outstanding example is that a secondary saline water (calcium & magnesium chlorides and sulfates) is incompatible with a primary alkaline water (Na$_2$CO$_3$, NaHCO$_3$).

Partial water analyses, easily made in the field, are often used to show what may be expected when different waters are mixed. The examples given in an accompanying table range from compatible at project 1, to black water at project 2, and to very pronounced barium sulfate scale at project 3. The incompatible compounds are marked by asterisks. It should be added that determination for dissolved oxygen would cause the mixture at project 1 to be corrosive. Also, some "red water" would be expected due to the iron content.

At project 2, corrosion would probably be severe, with only traces of dissolved oxygen, accompanied by accumulation of iron sulfide scale and corrosion products.

At project 3, entrained air would cause some corrosion and the resulting iron oxide would add to the build up of barium sulfate scale.

Water Chemistry—the Compounds Commonly in Solution in Natural Waters

Examples of "Partial Water Analysis" as a Quick Guide to Compatibility.

Project—	1		2		3	
	Produced brine	Supply water	Produced brine	Supply water	Produced brine	Supply water
mg/l						
SO$_4$	22	17	820	890	0	660*
Cl	77,600	57,180	13,150	5,020	104,700	69,170
HCO$_3$	125	120	740	550	50	45
Sp. Gr. 60/60°F	1.089	1.068	1.017	1.006	1.120	1.086
H$_2$S	NO	NO	290*	NO	NO	NO
Barium	NO	NO	NO	NO	640*	NO
Dissolved Fe	40	12	NO	55*	30	10

Conclusions: Project 1; compatible. Exclude air.
Project 2; incompatible, "black water."
Project 3; incompatible, BaSO$_4$ scale.

Several of the more common types of water are illustrated in the tables of water analyses, Tables 2, 3 and 4. The ionic form, in mg/l, is followed by Palmer values and finally by hypothetical combinations. In the following discussion, the analyses are described by number, emphasizing major characteristics or pointing out unusual constituents, so that the analysis "picture" will be fully complete.

TABLE 4. Brines Produced With Oil
Milligrams per liter (mg/l)

Analysis No.		12	13	14	15	16
		Sec. 25-6N-4E	Sec. 24-21S-34E	Sec. 24-20S-11W,	Sec. 2-24N-1W	Sec. 35-15N-4E
Sample		Okla.	N. Mex.	Kansas	Oklahoma	Mich.
Source		3375 ft.	3841 ft.	3310 ft.	4150 ft.	2840 ft.
	Na	4,869	3,085	7,500	66,933	75,709
Milli-	Ca	278	1,308	876	17,120	33,088
grams	Mg	102	676	370	2,248	7,670
per	SO$_4$	171	674	825	380	86
liter	Cl	7,800	7,446	13,150	139,720	197,570
	HCO$_3$	636	1,891	746	75	trace
	CO$_3$	nil	nil	nil	nil	nil
	Total Solids	13,856	15,080	23,467	226,476	314,123

WATER PROBLEMS IN OIL PRODUCTION
An Operator's Manual

Other constituents:

H₂S—	Yes	Yes	Yes	No	No
Dissolved iron—	trace	trace	trace	30 mg/l	14 mg/l
Sp.Gr. at 60°F—	1.010	1.009	1.017	1.155	1.217

Definition of Water Character (Palmer Values) in %

Primary Salinity	90.50	52.62	81.48	73.68	59.08
Secondary Salinity	5.04	35.22	15.46	26.30	40.92
Primary Alkalinity	0.00	0.00	0.00	0.00	0.00
Secondary Alkalinity	4.46	12.16	3.06	0.02	trace
	100.00%	100.00%	100.00%	100.00%	100.00%

Hypothetical Combination, A.P.H.A. Method of Calculation, mg/l

Ca(HCO₃)₂	846	2,514	991	99	trace
Mg(HCO₃)₂	—	—	—	—	—
NaHCO₃	—	—	—	—	—
CaCO₃	—	—	—	—	—
MgCO₃	—	—	—	—	—
Na₂CO₃	—	—	—	—	—
CaSO₄	234	954	1,168	537	122
MgSO₄	7	—	—	—	—
Na₂SO₄	—	—	—	—	—
CaCl₂	—	1,124	795	46,916	91,546
MgCl₂	393	2,632	1,448	8,800	30,025
NaCl	12,376	7,856	19,065	170,124	192,430
Total	13,856	15,080	23,467	226,476	314,123

Analysis No. 1 illustrates a rather hard, but potable water. "Temporary hardness," or bicarbonates, causing "teakettle scale" ($CaCO_3$) is predominant. However, some permanent hardness is also present. The latter consists of chlorides and sulfates of Ca and Mg.

Analysis No. 2 shows a very soft water, having primary alkalinity, Na_2CO_3, and $NaHCO_3$. This water is incompatible

Water Chemistry—the Compounds Commonly in Solution in Natural Waters

with all waters having secondary salinity, or Ca and Mg chlorides and sulfates, the same as permanent hardness. Although quite "soft," this water is not usually considered potable. It is harmless to fish and livestock, but good only for limited irrigation.

Analysis No. 3 is similar to No. 2, although much less salty. This water is excellent for all household purposes, livestock, irrigation, etc.

Analysis No. 4 proves that some very shallow well waters may be quite hard indeed. In addition to the high temporary and permanent hardness, this water has 5 mg/l of dissolved iron. Thus, it is unfit for household use but suitable for livestock and irrigation.

Analysis No. 5 is a good example of what is commonly termed "gyp" water. Note the calcium sulfate content. This water is unfit for household use and for irrigation. However, cattle use it and it is also harmless to fish.

The brackish waters and dilute brines set forth in Table 3 are all unfit for human consumption. Note that total hardness is not stated. This is usually quite significant in fresh waters but not in waters too saline for industrial or household uses. The formula for converting ionic calcium and magnesium to total hardness, as commonly stated in terms of $CaCO_3$, is as follows:

Total Hardness (as $CaCO_3$) = mg/l Ca × 2.50 + mg/l Mg × 4.115, dividing by 17.1 if grains per gallon is desired.

The water shown in Analysis No. 6 is used by livestock after H_2S has largely escaped to the atmosphere in an open pond. This water has a rather low hardness, but total solids of 6,000 mg/l are shown to be 72% by weight NaCl. The primary salinity of 79%, essentially all NaCl, reflects reacting value in % rather than the weight relationship. All the other waters, Table 3, are not suited to livestock, fish, and growing crops. Analyses No. 7 and No. 9 are "gyp" waters. No. 8 has barium which causes it to be incompatible with all waters having appreciable sulfate.

Analysis No. 9 is unusual in that it shows over 10,000 mg/l of sodium sulfate, Na_2SO_4. This is an illustration of how undesirable waters often occur in the Permian Red Beds. Obviously, the water with Na_2SO_4 is incompatible with any brines having appreciable calcium chloride, $CaCl_2$. This unfortunate mixture took place in the well, due to three zones being exposed. The resulting, enormous rate of gypsum accumulation is described in the succeeding chapter on scale formation.

Analysis No. 10 represents a flood supply water which caused corrosion and failure of the impeller in a turbine pump. This type of corrosion is common to sea water, which is portrayed by Analysis No. 11. The similarity between Analyses 10 and 11 is apparent.

The oilfield brines shown in Table 4 do not cover the wide range of salinity and character that are known to occur in the oil measures. For example, water produced with oil in some fields of Montana, Wyoming, New Mexico, California, and Venezuela is sometimes potable insofar as dissolved solids are concerned. The "calcium chloride" brines of Michigan are the most concentrated of known oilfield brines.

Brines of the oil formations are usually characterized by high primary salinity, with secondary salinity next in amount and secondary alkalinity limited to a few per cent. This is especially true in the north Midcontinent area, where the chlorides of sodium, calcium and magnesium make up 95% or more of the dissolved salts. However, primary alkaline waters are found in some of the more dilute oilwell brines of California, Venezuela and elsewhere.

Analysis No. 6, Table 3, is an isolated example of bicarbonate water. It is noteworthy that No. 6 water should not be mixed with No. 7 water before injection. Although all of the oil well brines listed show more or less gypsum in solution, this is not always so. Certain heavy brines contain barium and little or no sulfate. Mixtures of the barium-containing brines with sulfate brines will form hard, insoluble scales. The occurrence of calcium sulfate, much in excess of 2,000 mg/l,

Water Chemistry—the Compounds Commonly in Solution in Natural Waters

in some saline brines, exemplifies the increased solubility of high chloride brines for gypsum. This relationship is best set forth by the Gypsum Solubility Curve, Chart No. 1.

Many of the so-called "sweet" oilfield brines contain dissolved iron as produced. Somewhat more than 100 mg/l dissolved iron has been found in brine of the Bartlesville zone in central Oklahoma. This dissolved iron tends to precipitate on contact with air, illustrating one advantage of closed systems. Brines with appreciable dissolved iron are incompatible with brines having noticeable amounts of H_2S and such mixture should not take place before injection. The occurrence of "black water" in a sulfide-free system is justification for immediate tests to determine the presence of corrosive bacteria. This is treated in more detail under the subject of corrosion.

Space does not allow representation of all the characteristics to be found in the brines produced with oil, or all of the variations known to occur in fresh and brackish waters. However, most of the ordinary combinations are illustrated in the subjoined tables of analyses. The ionic statements reveal some outstanding contrasts between fresh waters and brines. An experienced water analyst recognizes these individual tendencies from the ionic statement alone.

The Palmer values and hypothetical combinations serve to bring the contrasts, or similarities, of given waters into clearer view for anyone having the equivalent of beginning chemistry. This fact was demonstrated by the very satisfactory progress made by trainee engineers, in a few hour's time, in the laboratory of a major oil company. With a minimum of attention given to these basic principles of water analysis, the non-chemist may gain the ability to recognize quickly the essential nature of a water and its probable reactions with another water. This understanding is possible from the ionic statement alone, or sometimes from an abbreviated statement of anions together with a single, significant cation.

At this point it is well to consider Table 5, setting forth the method of calculating a water analysis. The reader is urged to

WATER PROBLEMS IN OIL PRODUCTION
An Operator's Manual

spend sufficient thought on this calculation to become thoroughly familiar with it. In the absence of such preparation it is not possible to separate the wheat from the chaff in the many reports freely offered to waterflood operators. Following an understanding of the calculation, a re-examination of the analyses, Tables 2, 3 and 4 would be helpful. Now the contrasts in water characteristics stand out plainly and the reader is fully prepared to challenge "window dressing," errors in analysis and faulty interpretation.

In the following chapter on the formation of solid deposits, frequent reference will be made to certain water analyses in order to show clearly how the deposits are formed by the reactions of compounds in solution in waters of different nature.

REFERENCES

1. A.P.I. RP 45, Recommended Practice for Analysis of Oilfield Waters, Nov., 1965.
2. Drinking Water Standards. . . . Reprint No. 2440 from the Pub. Health Reports, vol. 58, no. 3, Jan., 1943.
3. F. W. Clarke, The Data of Geochemistry, 5th ed. U.S.G.S. Bull. 770, 1924.
4. Chemical Analyses of the Waters of Oklahoma. Pub. no. 52, Eng. Exp. Sta., Stillwater, Okla.
5. Herman Stabler, The Mineral Analysis of Water for Industrial Purposes and its Interpretation by the Engineer. Eng. News, vol. 60, 1908, p. 356. Also chap. on industrial App. of Water Analysis, U.S.G.S. Water Supply Paper 274, pp. 161–181.
6. Chase Palmer, The Geochemical Interpretation of Water Analyses. U.S.G.S. Bull. 479, 1911.
7. G. Sherburne Rogers, Chemical Relations of the Oil-Field Waters in San Joaquin Valley, Calif. U.S.G.S. Bull. 653, 1917. See also "Interpretation. . . ." Econ. Geol. vol. 12, 1917, pp. 56–88.
8. Eskel Nordell, Water Treatment for Industrial and Other Uses Reinhold Pub. Corp., N. Y., 1951.
9. L. C. Case, Application of Oil-Field Water Studies to Geology and Production. Oil Weekly, Oct. 29, 1945.
10. Manual on Industrial Water and Industrial Waste Water. 2d ed. 1960 printing. A.S.T.M. Philadelphia, Pa.

Water Chemistry—the Compounds Commonly in Solution in Natural Waters

TABLE 5. Derivation of a Balanced Water Analysis from the Essential Cations and Anions

Only 5 radicles are usually necessary in order to calculate a balanced analysis which may be subjected to meaningful interpretation. These may be obtained directly by tests, or sometimes recalculated from results in terms other than ionic values. The figures for sodium are found by difference, as follows, and the analysis completed.

	mg/l	e.p.l.*	e.p.l.%
Na	(10)	(0.45)	5.81
Ca	44	2.19	28.30
Mg	15	1.23	15.89
SO_4	21	0.43	5.55
Cl	32	0.90	11.63
HCO_3	158	2.54	32.82
CO_3	nil	nil	nil
Total	280	7.74	100.00%

* equivalents per liter = mg/l x reaction coefficient.

In the above analysis it will be seen that e.p.l. Ca + e.p.l. Mg = 3.42. Also, the sum of the anion e.p.l. is 3.87. Then the remaining cation e.p.l. is 0.45. This difference x atomic weight of Na = Na & K by difference, as Na.

If it is desired to obtain some idea as to the individual characteristics of this water, the Palmer values are found as follows, from e.p.l.%.

Primary Salinity: Alkalies + equal value of strong acids
    (Cl, SO_4)   11.62%
Secondary Salinity: Remaining strong acids + equal value of
    alkaline earths —   22.74
Primary Alkalinity: Alkalies + weak acids, not present —   0.00
Secondary Alkalinity: Remaining Alkaline earths + weak
    acids —   65.64
     100.00%

In the event that e.p.l. of alkalies is more than for strong acids, then no secondary salinity is present. Thus, e.p.l.% of strong acids × 2 = primary salinity. Remaining e.p.l.% of alkalies is balanced with weak acids to get primary alkalinity and remaining weak acids will exactly balance alkaline earths to obtain secondary alkalinity.

4

Solid Deposits— Scale Formation

It is the purpose of this chapter to set forth a clear and usable working explanation of scales and their prevention. The proper approach to such end may be achieved only by a few logical steps, in order, as follows:
1. Detection of the major constituents of the deposit.
2. Interpretation of cause, from above.
3. Confirmation of origin by examination of waters being mixed, or physical changes in a single water.
4. Recognition and consideration of physical methods of prevention, or
5. Selection of effective method for removal or treatment in the event that prevention at the source is not practical.

Solid deposits form mainly due to reactions between compounds in solution in the water being handled. Thus if the main components of a given scale are determined, the cause of the chemical precipitate is strongly indicated. Where different waters are being mixed, analyses of the waters before mixing confirms the origin of the scale. More rarely, a deposit may be due to "supersaturation," caused by physical changes rather than mixing incompatible water. Such changes are always made apparent by plant survey and certain tests on the water as it goes through the system.

The problem is often complicated by appreciable amounts of oil and corrosion products in the deposit. For this reason, it

Solid Deposits—Scale Formation

is almost always necessary to remove oil before making an examination of a sample of scale. Corrosion products are cause for alarm if they constitute an appreciable portion of a troublesome deposit. However, distinction must be made between inherent deposits of iron compounds and those due to the corrosion process.

In order to pursue this subject from a logical beginning, attention should be given to Table 6, which outlines an ap-

TABLE 6. Guide to Field Identification of Scales and Probable Causes.

Physical Appearance	Acid Solubility etc. (15% HCl)	Indicated Composition and Origin
1. White or light-colored:		
1.1 Hard, compact, fine granular	—Insoluble	$BaSO_4$, $SrSO_4$, $CaSO_4$—Incompatible waters.
1.2 Compact, with long, pearly crystals	—Powder dissolves slowly with no gas bubbles. Solution gives SO_4 test with $BaCl_2$.	Gypsum—$CaSO_4 \cdot 2 H_2O$. Incompatible waters or supersaturation.
1.3 Compact, fine gran. or crystals which break into rhombohedrons	—Easily sol. in HCl with gas bubbles.	$CaCO_3$ or mixture of $CaCO_3$ & $MgCO_3$ if more slowly dissolved. Supersaturation, rarely incompatible waters.
2. Dark Colored, brown to black:		
2.1 Compact, brown	—Essentially insol. brown color dissolves on heating. Acid turns yellow. White, insol. residue.	See 1.1 & 1.2 above for white residue. Brown, iron oxide is corrosion product or precipitate due to oxygen.
2.2 Compact, black	—Black mtl. dissolves slowly with	See 1.1 & 1.2 above for residue. Black color is

WATER PROBLEMS IN OIL PRODUCTION
An Operator's Manual

TABLE 6. (Cont.)

	evolution of H_2S, white, insoluble residue.	iron sulfide—corrosion product, incompat. waters, or both.
2.3 Compact, brown or black	—Easily sol. in 4% HCl (Dilute 15% 1:4) with gas bubbles. Brown or black color remains.	$CaCO_3$ with iron oxide or iron sulfide coloring matter.
2.4 Soft muck, usually brown or black:		
2.41	—Insoluble	See 1.1 above
2.42	—Dissolves, no bubbles	See 1.2 above
2.43	—Dissolves, gas bubbles	See 1.3 above
2.44	—Insoluble, except brown mtl., yellow solution	Iron oxide, se 2.1 above.
2.45	—Black material dissolves, evolution of H_2S	Iron sulfide, see 2.2 above.

Note: Discussion of inert residue and organic slime is omitted from the above outline. It should be emphasized that acid-insoluble residue occurs in all scale deposits, sometimes being the major ingredient. Also, "soft muck" deposits may contain all the others, in finely-divided state, and their recognition difficult due to more or less organic slime.

Usual Reaction of Compounds, in Solution in Water, to Form Solid Deposits

1. $BaCl_2 + Na_2SO_4 = BaSO_4 +$ 2 NaCl.......................... Barium sulfate, incompat. waters.
2. $SrCl_2 + MgSO_4 = SrSO_4 + MgCl_2$..... Strontium sulfate, as above
3. $CaCl_2 + Na_2SO_4 = CaSO_4 +$ 2 NaCl.......................... Gypsum, Incompat. waters or super sat.
4. $2\ NaHCO_3 + CaCl_2 = CaCO_3 +$ $2\ NaCl + CO_2 + H_2O$............... Calcium carbonate, by incompat. wtrs.
5. $Ca(HCO_3)_2 = CaCO_3 + CO_2 + H_2O$... Calcium carbonate, by supersat., due to pressure decrease, heat, agitation.

Solid Deposits—Scale Formation

6. $Fe + H_2S = FeS + H_2$ .... Corrosion. Iron sulfide may deposit or cause "black water."
7. $2\ Fe_2O_3 + 6\ H_2S = 2Fe_2S_3 + 6\ H_2O$ ... Inherent H_2S, or that from corrosive bacteria, combines with iron oxide in solution or suspension.

proach to field recognition of deposits and their origin. Admittedly, Table 6 constitutes an over-simplification of a problem which can be often quite complex, due to the many factors possibly involved. Nevertheless, the more common occurrences of deposits are described, together with probable causes, such that operators may distinguish between the obvious and the abstruse. Similarly, the need for competent investigation can be seen.

Perhaps the most important function of Table 6 is to point out that the deposits consist mainly of compounds originally present in solution, although these solid deposits may be modified in varying degrees by corrosion products, inert matter, organic slime and oil or emulsion. It is seldom possible to make a satisfactory examination of scale which is oil-soaked. After removal of most of the oil from compact scales, the criteria for tentative identification are usually made apparent by viewing with a hand lens and testing acid-solubility (oilfield grade HCl, approximately 15%).

The following descriptions will supplement the abbreviated discussion, Table 6.

1.1: Hard or compact scales of light color are necessarily sulfates of barium, strontium or calcium; or mixtures. If the powdered sample is insoluble in acid, then there is really no point in further analysis, or distinction between barium and strontium. The scale is due to a mixture of one water containing barium, or strontium, with another having sulfate. Initial analysis of the waters would have prevented this unfortunate mixture.

1.2: If the powder dissolves slowly with no effervescence, it

WATER PROBLEMS IN OIL PRODUCTION
An Operator's Manual

is probably gypsum. A sulfate test on the solution is confirmatory. Gypsum will precipitate due to a mixture of incompatible waters, Equation 3. When a water is saturated with gypsum, a decrease in temperature or slight evaporation may cause supersaturation and resultant, slow, accumulation of gypsum, at usual operating temperatures.

Chart 1 illustrates the increase of gypsum solubility with increased chloride content. This chart was originally drawn for relative values of SO_4 as Na_2SO_4, Ca as $CaCO_3$ and Cl as NaCl. The necessary conversion factors are therefore stated on the chart. This chart may be used with assurance when the points fall well to the left and below the NaCl lines, indicating negative gypsum formation; or to the right and above, indicating positive gypsum formation. However, if the Na_2SO_4-$CaCO_3$-NaCl values of a given water place its point in a critical area, the tendency to deposit gypsum should be fully checked by test nipples. One-inch, removable nipples, placed near a meter serve well for this purpose. In the event of needle-like "whiskers" appearing on the interior of the test nipple in 2–3 weeks, operating under average conditions, near-term trouble from gypsum may be confidently predicted.

It should be clearly understood that the "Stiff Index," for calculating tendency of waters to deposit gypsum, is of little value. This index indicated a certain brine to be harmless from the standpoint of gypsum precipitation. Nevertheless, a deposit of crystalline gypsum, approximately 1 in. in thickness, formed on the pump screen and shaft in a period of 25 days of normal operation. Breakage of the pump shaft was the signal for realization of the deposit. All conditions attendant to this gypsum formation, failure of the "index" and its obvious omissions were published,[5] and the data have never been invalidated or controverted in any way.

Additionally, Metler and Ostroff[14] have illustrated conclusively the serious errors of the Stiff and Davis method[15] by actual laboratory measurements.

Even so, outspoken approval of the index has been noted at

Solid Deposits—Scale Formation

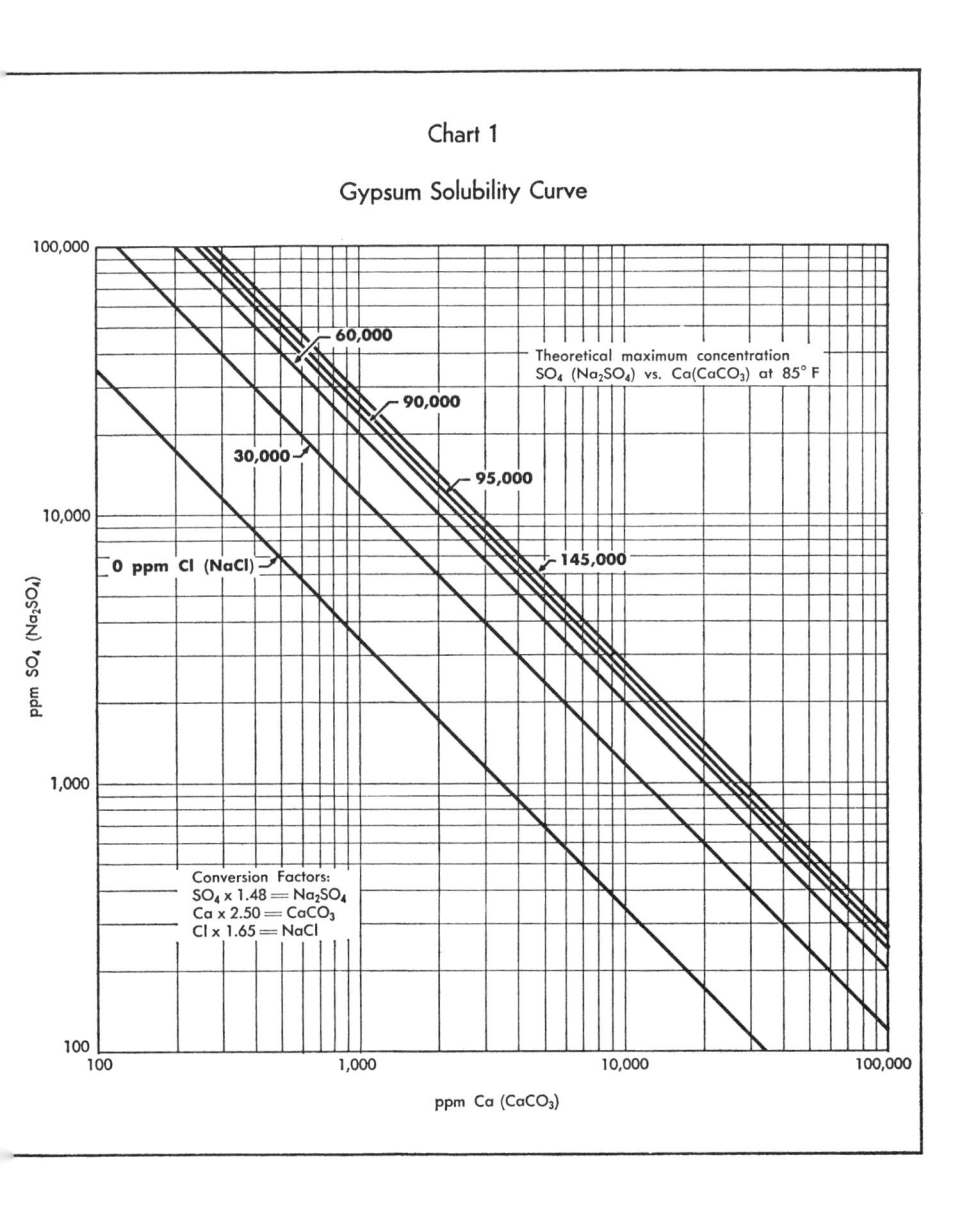

Chart 1

Gypsum Solubility Curve

Theoretical maximum concentration SO$_4$ (Na$_2$SO$_4$) vs. Ca(CaCO$_3$) at 85° F

Curves labeled: 0 ppm Cl (NaCl), 30,000, 60,000, 90,000, 95,000, 145,000

Y-axis: ppm SO$_4$ (Na$_2$SO$_4$), from 100 to 100,000
X-axis: ppm Ca (CaCO$_3$), from 100 to 100,000

Conversion Factors:
SO$_4$ x 1.48 = Na$_2$SO$_4$
Ca x 2.50 = CaCO$_3$
Cl x 1.65 = NaCl

recent, technical meetings. Such is the power of the printed word when it is left unchallenged for too many years. It would seem an understatement to conclude that anyone offering proof of gypsum trouble and need for preventive treatment, based on this index or similar calculations, should be suspect of incompetence in the field of water problems.

1.3,2.3 Calcium carbonate is attacked by dilute HCl with vigorous evolution of CO_2. Dilute the common, oilfield grade HCl, 1 part acid to 3 parts water. If not too protected by very heavy oil, the $CaCO_3$ will dissolve quickly in the approximate 4% acid. $MgCO_3$ dissolves much more slowly and iron sulfide not at all. The use of 15% or stronger HCl sometimes evolves much H_2S gas from sulfides in the deposits and may lead to false conclusions as to carbonates.

If a system is handling black water, due to suspended sulfide, and also has appreciable $CaCO_3$ scale, the latter will be quite black from the occluded sulfide. As little as 1% iron sulfide in carbonate deposits will have this effect. Carbonate scales are usually due to supersaturation, or loss of CO_2, Equation 5. However, incompatible waters may throw down carbonate, Equation 4. Another example is that a fresh water, highly charged with bicarbonate, when added to a saline brine will rapidly deposit $CaCO_3$.

2.1,2.2 The sulfate deposits may be masked completely by oxides, sulfides, muck or inert matter. It is thus necessary to examine the residue from acid digestion, using strong acid—15% or more. Iron sulfide dissolves slowly, with bubbles and the familiar odor of H_2S. Iron oxide requires longer to dissolve. Magnetic iron oxide will dissolve only with heat and standing for some time. The latter material is easily identified with a small magnet.

2.4 Any decision as to constitution and cause of soft and slimy "muck," based on field tests, is subject to considerable error and should be avoided. Such "goop" may contain small amounts of all the other types of deposits, plus organic slime, oil, or emulsion and various kinds of inert matter. Rather accomplished chemists have been known to fail miserably when making analyses and stating the origin of unconsolidated deposits in waterflood systems. It is indeed fortunate when an accumulation of this kind is found to consist mainly of one material—which in turn will respond to easy correction.

If this sort of material is blackflowed from injection wells, this should be the sampling point. A few milligrams, collected on a membrane filter from the injection stream, does not compare as a respresentative sample, although the latter is better than no sample at all. Infrequently, simple tests, such as color, acid solubility, smell, and elutriation of inert matter will give some idea of the main material and its cause. More often, the sample should be protected from contact with air and sent to an experienced analyst, who should report the several components in % dry weight.

Preparation of sample for analysis includes removal of oil, water-soluble salts and water. This is followed by estimation of the solid materials, Table 6, organic matter and inert material. The latter should be identified as sand, clay, etc., rather than merely "inert" or "siliceous sediment." It will be seen that total elemental content, such as Na,Ca, Ba,Sr,Cl,Fe, etc., as reported by spectrographic analysis, has no interpretative value. Moreover, when the solids are known and reported in their state of occurrence, the causes of formation are revealed. All the solid deposits, except the complex, soft, and usually non-adherent ones, lend themselves to rather positive identification.

Certain problems demand a little extra attention. For example, "black water," or suspended iron sulfide, may be due to corrosion by indigenous sulfide, corrosion by H_2S from SO_4-reducing bacteria, or to iron sulfide precipitation caused by mixing a sulfide water with an iron-containing water. Here the significant tests would consist of examination of all waters prior to mixing and systematic tracing of the sources of the iron and sulfide. Simple logic dictates that supply water and produced brine, initially free of sulfide, should not carry suspended iron sulfide. If it does, then tests for corrosive bacteria show the cause.

Tests for dissolved iron in produced brine may be considered, in conjunction with the growth of corrosive bacteria through the system, when tracing the source of the iron in black water. These data should confirm the existing corrosion rate, which is usually apparent at most plants.

The procedure for identification of basic causes of scale accumulation is never the same at different waterfloods. The approach must be comprehensive, yet variable in view of existing conditions. Thus, short cuts to meaningful data are usually available.

For example, if completely compatible, sulfide-free waters are being mixed at a given flood, with oxygen excluded, then all the solid deposits would be eliminated from consideration. Black water would signal the need for bug tests, cleaning out the system, and preventive treatment. Additional solutions are quickly apparent when unstable water is being "cascaded" into an open tank ahead of injection pumps, or when dirty pond water is being continuously added to a volume tank.

The physical methods of scale prevention are much preferred, since there is only a first cost, rather than continued expense of chemical additives. The possible, physical, preventives may be broadly stated as follows:

1. Separation of incompatible waters. (See design for split system, appendix).
2. Prevention of conditions causing supersaturation.
3. Elimination of air entry.
4. Use of settling or filtration to remove inert matter.

These preventives may require certain changes in plant equipment after a period of operation. However, many of the preventives may be included in design if conditions are surveyed prior to plant construction.

Chemical removal of deposits is sometimes practical. This is more especially true for injection wells than for surface

Solid Deposits—Scale Formation

equipment. It is almost axiomatic that treatment with hydrochloric acid is more universally successful than all other chemical methods of removal. The acid may be used with detergent to aid in attack on oily materials, with sequestering agents to hold up dissolved iron, etc. With acid-insoluble deposits, i.e., $BaSO_4$, $CaSO_4$, the use of "Versene," or "E.D.T.A." may be beneficial. Comprehensive coverage of the subject of cleaning deposits would require a great deal of space, at the possible risk of loss of reader interest. Additional discussion of specific problems will be given in the chapter devoted to the location and correction of operating difficulties.

Chemical methods for preventing the solid deposits are limited to the use of sequestering agents. The so-called "stabilization" process, consisting of coagulation, settling in open basins, and filtration has proved expensive, difficult to control and generally impractical. Sequestering agents were first used to prevent precipitation of calcium carbonate. Sodium hexametaphosphate served well for this purpose. The use of mixtures of the solid polyphosphates, with certain "synergistic" additives, was broadened and applied to prevention of the sulfate deposits.

Although usually successful when properly used, the solid polyphosphates have the disadvantage of being difficult to feed in required amounts. Polyphosphates which are quite slowly soluble have been used with some success for downhole application and prevention of scale in subsurface equipment. Ideally, the placement of 100 lb or so of this material will last 6 months to 1 year. However, the rate of solution of the solid polyphosphates cannot be stated for any given brine. It follows that check tests for residual metaphosphate (PO_3) must be made periodically on well effluent. It has been observed that the suppliers of the slowly-soluble polyphosphates are extremely lax in following through on promises of regular check tests.

The surface usage of solid polyphosphates requires frequent manual dosage or the use of solutions. The latter are objectionable due to usual absence of suitable water, freezing of solutions, and reversion to orthophosphate, PO_4, which is ineffective. Quite recently, liquid organic polyphosphates have successfully invaded the field of scale prevention. At least 5 companies in good standing now offer as many liquid polyphosphates for preventing solid deposits. Some of these have been found effective, even on the hard, sulfate scales, in amounts as low as 15 ppm.

Certain of these preventives work better than others where the scaling compounds are present in high concentration. This, and other factors relating to efficacy and cost, should be obtained from all possible sources before field use of the liquid scale preventives. Presently, the available records of field use strongly indicate that the liquid materials are superior, both in results and overall cost. One or more field examples of scale prevention by sequestering agents will be outlined in Chapter 8.

ESTIMATION OF SCALING TENDENCY

Useful limits of the "Gypsum Solubility Curve" have been previously outlined. Methods for calculating more exact inclination of waters to throw down gypsum have been needed for many years. Long term experience and good memory as to the effects of salinity and temperature have been somewhat helpful in predictions relating to gypsum formation. This "rule of thumb" method is ordinarily improved to some degree by hypothetical combinations. These may indicate gypsum deposits at the expected operating temperature when the gypsum solubility curve fails to do so.

Thus, it seems that predictions concerning gypsum precipitation have long been an undependable art, at best. More than 45 years of salt water disposal and waterflood practice constitute proof of the statement. However, relatively recent attention to the problem by competent physical chemists has

Solid Deposits—Scale Formation

strongly indicated that prediction of gypsum deposits may at last become a science.

Reference to one outstanding recent work is given in the accompanying table.

GYPSUM DUE TO MIXING OF UNLIKE WATERS
Analyses, mg/l

Source—	Supply Water, deep well	Supply Water, shallow well
Na	60,596	1,519
Ca	9,248	379
Mg	1,392	196
SO_4	739	3,908
Cl	113,184	616
HCO_3	210	146
Total Solids	185,369	6,764

Hypothetical Combinations

$Ca(HCO_3)_2$	275	194
$CaSO_4$	1,048	1,126
$MgSO_4$	0	970
Na_2SO_4	0	3,458
$CaCl_2$	24,573	0
$MgCl_2$	5,454	0
NaCl	154,019	1,016
Total	185,369	6,764

Conclusion: Preliminary charting of these values indicates that gypsum will be thrown down due to any degree of mixing. However, extensive calculations show that up to 40% of the shallow supply water may be mixed, with no scale resulting. Reference: A. V. Metler & A. G. Ostroff, Environ. Sci. & Tech. Oct., 1967.

Soon after publication of the first edition of this book, a problem was encountered with supply water at a very large waterflood. The waters of the shallow and deep supply wells in the accompanying table were definitely incompatible. The supply from either well was inadequate. Thus, it became necessary to employ a more precise method of estimating gypsum formation.[14] The method cited by Metler and Ostroff uses formulas derived for the calculation of gypsum solubility in various concentrations of Na, Mg, Ca, Cl and SO_4 ions at

WATER PROBLEMS IN OIL PRODUCTION
An Operator's Manual

28°, 38°, 59° and 70°C. Corrections are included for a wide range of excess Ca or SO_4, and the results are substantiated by comprehensive laboratory determinations of solubility in brines of varying salt content.

Using this method, it was found that up to 40% of the shallow water could be mingled above ground with the deep supply water. This result obviated a split injection system. However, in this case it was strongly recommended to the operator that the return brine be continually checked before mixing with the composite injection brine.

No attempt is made here to shorten or simplify the necessary calculation used in the Metler-Ostroff example. Reference to the complete work and its familiarity are essential to practical use of the method. It follows that the average chemical salesman, or even field petroleum engineer, is not capable of using the rather advanced chemistry and mathematics involved.

In regard to calcium carbonate deposits in brines, it may be said that the criteria are even less exact than for gypsum. Although rather precise calculations have been established for waters of low total solids, these calculations may not be extrapolated to oilfield brines with any degree of accuracy. Here again, a knowledge of certain fundamental values in a water analysis may serve as a warning as to carbonate deposits in a brine system. For example, we know of the close relationship between carbon dioxide and bicarbonate in water. The former is difficult to determine accurately in a brine. However, if the pH goes up, or HCO_3 goes down, while standing at room temperature for a short time, it is a safe bet that the brine will throw down a certain amount of carbonate scale.

In rare cases, the pH of brines will go down on heating due to the hydrolysis of organic salts sometimes found in oil field brines. Usually however, release of pressure, slight heating, or agitation serve to release the CO_2 which holds the calcium bicarbonate in solution. Unfortunately, we cannot determine bottom-hole pH and alkalinity values. These may be calcu-

Solid Deposits—Scale Formation

lated, but the required data are difficult to obtain, and results are generally believed to be inexact. Although well-head determinations often indicate a stable brine, appreciable carbonate may be accumulating near the bottom of the well bore, or point of initial pressure decrease. Such condition is normally accompanied by more or less carbonate deposition between well head and other surface equipment. Mechanical removal is preferred when cleaning becomes necessary, since chemical cleaning is slow and expensive. Scale preventive has proved useful and economical when unstable brine is re-injected.

In summary, it should be clearly stated that any "scaling index" based on laboratory tests of brine samples, not kept under operating conditions, is totally devoid of any significance. Numerical statements of scaling index have been noted in various reports concerning brine handling systems. In all cases, inquiry revealed that the analyst did not have sufficient experience to understand the chemical constitution of brines and that he could neither explain nor defend the derivation of the index.

Any discussion of carbonate scaling tendency should include a practical explanation of the long-established "Saturation Index" and the more recent "Stability Index." These Indexes [6,7] employ rather precise equations for calculating the tendency of dilute waters to deposit or dissolve calcium carbonate.

The "Calcium Carbonate Saturation Index" was originally compiled by Dr. W. F. Langelier as the algebraic difference between the actual pH of a water and its calculated pH value. The latter, or "pH$_s$," is actually the logarithm of the degree of carbonate saturation. Some rather practical additions to the original equations (See References 8, 9, 10, 11) have included corrections for temperature and total solids, but the latter do not include brines.

Readily available charts or diagrams may be used to short cut the calculations and thus obtain the Saturation Index, commonly referred to as the "Langelier Index." Stated most

WATER PROBLEMS IN OIL PRODUCTION
An Operator's Manual

simply, this is actual pH minus calculated pH (pH$_s$). Determined values for alkalinity, calcium, and total solids are necessary for calculating pH$_s$. When deducting pH$_s$ from actual pH, a plus value shows a tendency to deposit CaCO$_3$ and a minus value a tendency to dissolve it. The calculation is only qualitative, also undependable where the plus or minus values are less than unity.

For example, a water with a saturation index of minus 0.1 will often change to plus 0.2 with a temperature rise of 20°F. For practical purposes, the scaling tendency is usually dependable when found +0.5 or above and the temperature of operation is known. A similar relationship does not exist for minus values and the incidence of corrosion. Usually, such values reflect only a tendency to dissolve CaCO$_3$ at the given temperature. This, in turn, is due to "aggressive CO$_2$" which may be corrosive but usually is merely additive to oxygen or sulfide corrosion.

Carbon dioxide injection at a number of waterfloods has shown generally that CO$_2$ is not corrosive in the absence of oxygen, organic acids, and possibly certain amounts of H$_2$S. At one unusual flood, a fresh water highly charged with CO$_2$ constituted the supply. It was necessary to put this supply water through a baffled separator to remove much of the gas before pumping to injection wells.

Brine produced with the oil had 10-20 mg/l of H$_2$S. A mixture of return brine and fresh water supply was injected in the absence of dissolved oxygen. Inspection of injection lines after 5 years of operation showed only a thin, black coating on the interior of the lines, with no pits or perforations.

A somewhat more usable index has been proposed by Dr. J. W. Ryznar.[7] Although derived from the same calculations for solubility equilibria, the "Stability Index," commonly called the "Ryznar Index," provides a semi-quantitative estimate of scale which may be formed or often a qualitative prediction of corrosion. This is arrived at by assigning more importance to the calculated pH of CaCO$_3$ saturation, as follows.

Stability Index = $2pH_s$ minus pH. Selected examples illustrate the different viewpoints afforded by saturation index and stability on two different waters.

Water No. 1: At 120°F, pH_s = 6.0, actual pH = 6.5 and saturation index = +0.5

Water No. 2: At 120°F, pH_s = 9.0, actual pH = 9.5 and saturation index = +0.5

Using the above waters, the indexes are compared as follows.

	Saturation Index	Stability Index
Water No. 1:	+0.5	+5.5
Water No. 2:	+0.5	+8.5

It may be seen that the saturation index is identical for the two waters and somewhat misleading in that it does not reflect any difference in values for calcium and total alkalinity. The latter values are included when actual pH is deducted from $2pH_s$ to obtain stability index. All values for the latter are positive and, in general, waters having a stability index of 5.5 will form appreciable scale; while a water of index 8.5 will form little if any scale and may be corrosive, especially at higher temperatures. A recently published circular slide rule facilitates the calculation of stability index for dilute waters.[12]

REFERENCES

1. L. W. Jones, Development of a Mineral Scale Inhibitor. Corrosion, vol. 17, no. 5, 1961.
2. Joe R. Wright, Methods for Determining Characteristics of Water Used in the Petroleum Industry. Oil and Gas Jour., June 23, July 14 and Sept. 15, 1945.
3. A. G. Ostroff, Introduction to Oilfield Water Technology, Prentice-Hall, 1965.
4. L. C. Case, Scales in Oil-Producing Equipment. Oil and Gas Jour., Sept. 28, 1946.
5. L. C. Case, Watch Those Mixed Injection Waters. Oil and Gas Jour., Aug. 8, 1960.
6. W. F. Langelier, The Analytical Control of Anti-Corrosion Wa-

ter Treatment. Jour. Am. Waterworks Assoc., vol. 28, no. 10, 1936.
7. J. W. Ryznar, A New Index for Determining Amount of Calcium Carbonate Scale Formed by a Water. Jour. Am. Waterworks Assoc. vol. 36, no. 4, 1944.
8. T. E. Larson and A. M. Buswell, Calcium Carbonate Saturation Index and Alkalinity Interpretations. Jour. Am. Waterworks Assoc. vol. 34, 1942.
9. C. P. Hoover, Practical Application of the Langelier Method. Jour. Am. Waterworks Assoc., vol. 30, 1938.
10. A. A. Hirsch, A Special Slide Rule for Calcium Carbonate Equilibrium Problems, Ind. and Eng. Chem., Anal. Ed., 1942.
11. A. A. Hirsch, Scalar Diagram for pH of Calcium Carbonate Equilibrium, Journal Am. Waterworks Assoc., vol. 35, 1943.
12. Nalco Aquagraph, copyright 1959, Nalco Chemical Company.
13. J. F. Tate, R. L. Venable, and C. C. Nathan. Division of Petroleum Chemistry, 148th Meeting ACS, Chicago, Ill., Aug., 1964.
14. A. V. Metler and A. G. Ostroff, The Proximate Calculation of the Solubility of Gypsum in Natural Brines from 28° to 70° C. Environmental Science and Technology, Vol. 1, No. 10, Oct., 1967.
15. H. A. Stiff, L. E. Davis. J. Pet. Tech. 4(2), 25-8, 1952.

5
Corrosion Causes, Prevention, and Treatment

All corrosion taking place in the presence of an electrolyte may be stated to be more or less electrochemical in nature. However, the science of cathodic protection will be excluded from this discussion. The corrosion commonly occurring in water handling systems consists mainly of acid gas attack. Acid gas corrosion is caused, for the most part, by H_2S. No doubt CO_2 causes some corrosion, especially when aided by dissolved oxygen. However, the comparative effect of CO_2 has been grossly over-emphasized. It should be noted in this connection that in the process of using CO_2 in injection water, all available reports mention slight scaling with calcium carbonate in producing wells, but deny any appreciable corrosion. In further proof of the negligible effect of CO_2, the following summary of operations at one flood should be noted.

The subject flood used a mixed injection water, consisting of dilute, produced brine, containing approximately 10 mg/l of H_2S and a fresh supply water having an excessive amount of CO_2. It was necessary to run the supply water through a baffled separator, on the way to the mixing tank, so that some CO_2 gas was removed and the injection pumps would operate efficiently. The system was oxygen-free. The expected corrosion due to the acid gases did not take place. On the contrary, there were no failures in unprotected injection lines or tubing in 6 years of operation. An inspection showed a thin, continu-

WATER PROBLEMS IN OIL PRODUCTION
An Operator's Manual

ous film of iron sulfide on the interior of the lines, which obviously served as a protective coating.

In general, water which contains CO_2 in addition to low amounts of dissolved oxygen, is more corrosive, due mainly to the lower pH which is caused by the CO_2. Such a mixture can be appreciably more corrosive than equal total concentrations of oxygen and CO_2 acting alone. This synergistic effect is not present at high oxygen amounts with low CO_2 amounts. The apparently anomalous relationship is possibly explained by difference in nature of the corrosion film which is formed. The lower corrosion rate with high oxygen: low CO_2 contents has been utilized in a practical manner in certain lines carrying fresh water and where tuberculation is evident. Under these conditions, the tuberculation is due to relatively high CO_2 and low oxygen in the water. Aeration of the water reverses the ratio and stops the attack.

It has been shown conclusively that CO_2 does not accelerate the attack by H_2S in a brine. Rather, corrosion by H_2S in brines is usually lessened by the presence of CO_2. Again, this seems to be due to the nature of the protective film formed by the corrosion products.

There are no criteria for easy field recognition of CO_2 corrosion. The products of CO_2 attack are water-soluble and thus do not remain on metal surfaces or in pits. It follows that any effect of CO_2 must be found by careful tests for pH and for the gas itself. Additionally, these values must be accompanied by other determinations for possible effects of H_2S and dissolved oxygen. Certain physical factors such as temperature and velocity may also be pertinent.

Corrosion attack by H_2S may be due to that gas occurring naturally in the brine, or to sulfide produced by corrosive bacteria, or to both causes. There are no dependable criteria for preventing this type of corrosion, such as maximum permissible H_2S, water characteristics, etc. Field practice shows

Corrosion Causes, Prevention, and Treatment

PLATE 1. Thick scale in 2 in. injection line. Pitting attack is severe underneath scale, causing 2.5 line leaks per injection well/month. Pits under the ½-in. thick scale were filled with iron sulfide corrosion product at all stages up to complete perforation.

WATER PROBLEMS IN OIL PRODUCTION
An Operator's Manual

PLATE 2. Graphitic Corrosion. Impeller from turbine pump which failed in service due to brackish water being handled.

Corrosion Causes, Prevention, and Treatment

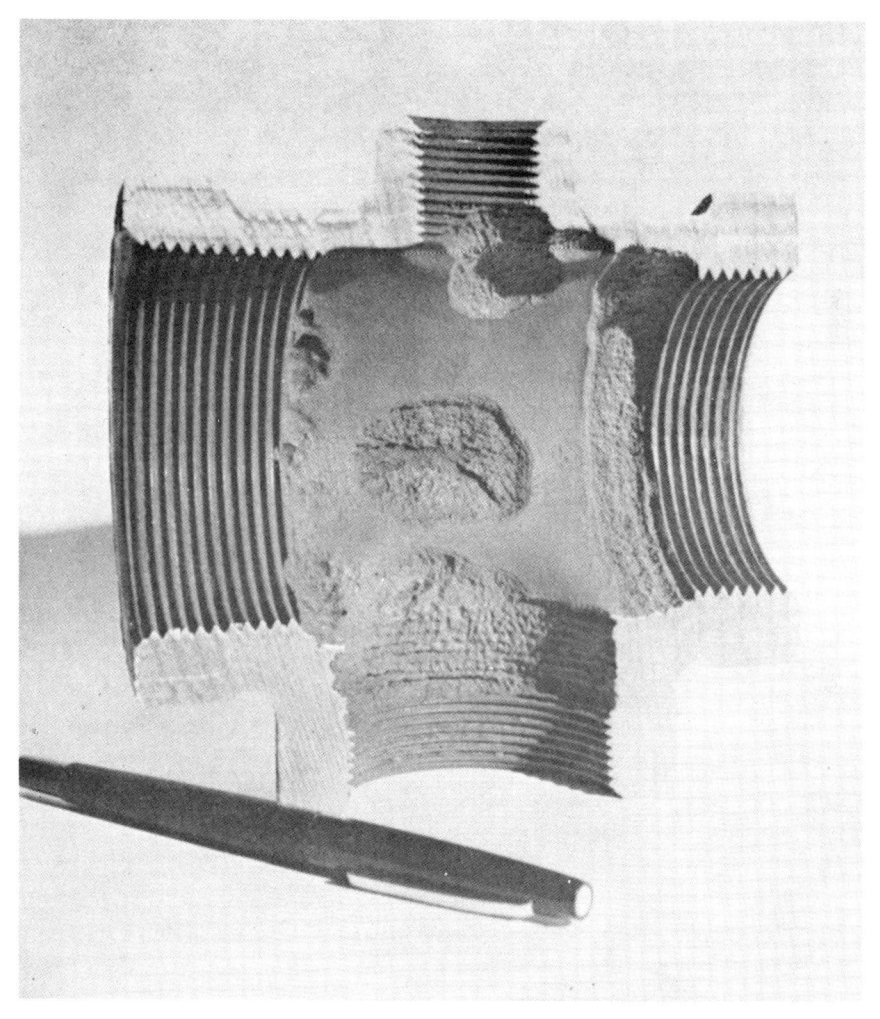

PLATE 3. Sweet-oil (organic acid) corrosion in Oklahoma. This is rare in the north Mid-Continent area, though rather common in condensate wells and farther south. This occurred is the Skinner Sand, Lincoln County. It should be noted that these corroded areas were washed out as removed, rather than filled with corrosion product.

WATER PROBLEMS IN OIL PRODUCTION
An Operator's Manual

PLATE 4. Carbon dioxide corrosion on a rod box from Smackover field, southern Arkansas. This, along with organic-acid corrosion, is classed as sweet-oil corrosion.

that 100 mg/l of H_2S or more is only mildly corrosive in the dilute brines of west Texas and New Mexico when oxygen is excluded. On the other hand, much less sulfide, in slightly more saline brines, is very corrosive in western Kansas.

Under-scale corrosion is primarily due to H_2S attack. This type of corrosion can and does occur under thick scale deposits, which serve to localize the corrosion, rather than to protect the steel surfaces. No outward evidence, such as black water or free sulfide, may usually be noted when this is taking place in a system using "sweet" water. Normally, the appearance of iron sulfide, or any free H_2S, is cause for immediate alarm. However, these convenient signs may not be apparent when the attack is concentrated to very small areas under heavy scale.

The basic cause, sulfide-producing bacteria, tend to proliferate under any sort of protective cover and in crevices. The liberated H_2S attacks the steel, causing a pit, which grows at an ever increasing rate. In this example, galvanic corrosion is induced by a current flowing from the steel (anode) to the iron sulfide corrosion product. This type of pitting by localized H_2S attack is not limited to sweet brine systems. Rather, it usually takes place in any system, sweet or sour, where scale is allowed to accumulate. The situation is so common and so destructive that the frequent admonition "get rid of the scale first" should be given serious consideration. Refer to Plate 1 for a most remarkable example of under-scale corrosion.

Tuberculation corrosion is very similar to under scale corrosion. The process is the same except that tuberculation is usually limited to smaller areas, and is thus less severe. The tubercles are small mounds of scale attached to the metal surface. Tuberculation usually occurs in fresh water or dilute brines which contain dissolved oxygen and are also unstable as to carbonate saturation. Thus the nodules are normally composed of mixed carbonates and hydrated iron oxides. Although tubercles may sometimes herald the beginning of thick scale deposits, they are more often innocuous, except for the growth of corrosive bacteria at their bases.

The black sulfide cores, noted when prying off the nodules with the point of a knife, occupy active pits which vary in size with that of the sulfide cores. Cultures of the bacteria in the tubercles have confirmed the mechanism, but the bacteria are not necessary for recognition of tuberculation and pitting attack. In a medium of little oxygen, the tubercles sometimes consist of red or yellow iron oxide on the outside and magnetic iron oxide at the base. The tubercles may become dislodged and the pits swept clean of corrosion product for a time, but repeated, more often than otherwise, in the same spot; thus producing deep pits and pipe perforation.

Oxygen corrosion, per se, is somewhat rare since brines do not ordinarily contain oxygen and the corrosion in fresh water due to dissolved oxygen is usually quite mild. Additionally, oxygen corrosion in fresh water responds to economical treatment with inhibitors, which is not true of oxygen corrosion in brines, either sweet or sour. Oxygen has been shown by lab and field tests to be corrosive in sweet brines when present in amounts of 0.3—0.5 mg/l. This is chemical attack, and the corrosion products are red or brown iron oxides. In sour brines the effect of dissolved oxygen is not apparent because the corrosion products are almost always entirely black, with no oxides in evidence. The acceleration of sulfide corrosion by dissolved oxygen is said to be due to depolarization of the sulfide-filmed steel surface. This causes at least a portion of the film to become loosened, whereupon the attack is repeated rapidly. The magnitude of the oxygen influence will be realized best by brief consideration of corrosion history at a west Texas waterflood.

Injection water at this flood contained in excess of 200 mg/l H_2S. However, corrosion rate was determined by coupons to be in the order of 2–4 M.P.Y. at the startup. A few months later the rate was measured by coupons to be 100 M.P.Y. or greater at certain points in the system near the occurrence of pipe failures. Extensive investigation revealed entry of air, at or near the points of failure, such that the sour brine at times contained as much as 0.4 mg/l of dissolved oxygen. The obvious conclusion is that air should be rigorously excluded from sour systems. If it were possible to measure, with dependable accuracy, as little as 0.01 mg/l of dissolved oxygen in an unprotected system using sour water, this result would serve as a guarantee of near-term trouble from corrosion.

Aeration cells, sometimes called oxygen concentration cells, are due to small amounts of dissolved oxygen and cause localized pitting similar in many respects to under-scale corrosion. Aeration cells are electrolytic cells, the emf being due to differences in oxygen concentration at one electrode as compared with that of another electrode of the same material. Thus, these cells occur in crevices or on steel surfaces in loose contact with steel or other material. The phenomenon may be observed on coupons, under the fasteners which hold the steel plates to the plastic rods.

Another example is the use of rubber bands on coupons, in an attempt to create aeration cells, thus indicating presence or absence of oxygen. The pitting caused by aeration cells is similar in appearance to corrosion occurring under scales. Prevention is best accomplished by total exclusion of air. Inhibitor and biocides are generally unable to reach the affected areas. However, chemicals with detergent characteristics are sometimes found helpful.

Galvanic corrosion, or "bimetallic corrosion," may take place in any system handling brine where steel and non-ferrous metals are in contact. Reasons for this are usually obvious and prevention simple. One often-repeated admonition reflects rather wide recognition of the general principles of galvanic corrosion; "Do not screw a steel plug into a bronze pump housing or expect steel pipe nipples to last when connected to bronze meters without insulation."

The latter conditions represent prime examples of unfavorable metal area ratios. The extensive explanation given in many corrosion publications may be stated briefly for practical application.

The high conductivity of brines lessens galvanic corrosion where the dissimilar metal relationships are favorable. A high ratio of anodic (steel) area to cathodic (brass, bronze, etc.) area results in a low anodic current density. For this reason, brass, bronze, Monel, or stainless steel trimmed cast iron fittings and valves give good service in brines. Similarly, Monel and stainless welds may be used on steel since the relative area of noble metal is small.

On the other hand, large areas of noble metal should not be coupled to small areas of steel, as with the steel plug in a bronze pump housing. A closely similar condition to be avoided would consist of using steel rivets to fasten bronze or brass structures in a salt water system.

Finally, it should be emphasized that it is impractical to protect anodic (steel) areas, where area of noble metal is greater, by painting or coating the steel. Any failure of the coating, however small, produces a current density of such intensity that failure is immediate. In other words, if a condition accidentally occurs where the steel shell of a vessel is endangered by nearby large areas of copper, bronze, or brass tubes, it would be best to heed the textbook advice and "paint the cathode."

Graphitic corrosion of cast iron takes the form of local attack along the boundaries of the graphite flakes and the iron. This is due to the fact that graphite is strongly cathodic to iron. The action proceeds in saline waters until there is little left but the graphite and the corrosion products which form a pseudomorph of the original metal. This type of corrosion occurs more commonly in corrosive soils or brackish waters, particularly those which carry calcium sulfates or chlorides.

Numerous examples of graphitic corrosion occur in sea water and in soils along the coast. The impeller from the turbine pump, Plate 2, is truly a "textbook example" of the process described above. It should be noted that the water handled by the pump, Analysis 10, Table 3, is rather similar in salinity and sulfate content to sea water. The example of the turbine pump impeller serves to illustrate the wisdom of not using cast iron in salt water service. Refer to "Guide for Selection of Metals," Appendix.

Sweet oil corrosion, caused by organic acids rather than by H_2S, is common in condensate wells but relatively unusual in pumping oil wells. Only one occurrence of sweet oil corrosion has been reported in Oklahoma waterflood operations. Attack by the organic acid took place in lead lines of pumping wells. The producing wells were being flooded by a near-perfect injection brine—free of H_2S and dissolved oxygen. The increased corrosion rate, corresponding to increased ratio of produced brine, led to isolation of organic acids in the produced brine.

Corrosion attack by the organic acids caused very deep pits of large size. These pits were free of corrosion product since the organic salts of iron are relatively soluble. Although the pits were similar in appearance to pits originating from impingement attack, they were not limited to areas of turbulence. Physical appearance of "sweet oil corrosion pitting" can be only an indication, at best. Only chemical tests are dependable as to the presence of organic acids. Effective remedies consist of continuous use of inhibitor or coating the pipe.

REFERENCES

1. Frank N. Speller, Corrosion Causes and Prevention (3rd ed.) McGraw-Hill Book Co., Inc., 1951.

WATER PROBLEMS IN OIL PRODUCTION
An Operator's Manual

2. A. G. Ostroff, Introduction to Oilfield Water Technology, Prentice-Hall, Inc., 1965.
3. H. H. Uhlig (ed.) The Corrosion Handbook, John Wiley & Sons, Inc., 1948.
4. L. C. Case and W. C. Whiteside, Less Oxygen = Less Corrosion, Oil & Gas Jour., Oct. 20, 1958.
5. L. C. Case, Will Corrosion Eat Up the Waterflood Profit? Oil & Gas Jour., Jan. 16, 1961.

6

Plugging or Fouling Deposits

A great deal of confusion exists concerning the slimy material which sometimes becomes noticeable in waterflood systems. The actual makeup and causes of this sort of accumulation are usually misunderstood or largely disregarded. It is a rather common practice of some investigators to make a few bacteria tests, relate the deposits to prolific microorganisms, and prescribe chemical treatment accordingly.

It should be recognized that plugging material, consisting mainly of living or dead microorganisms, is quite rare indeed. When this does take place, there are a number of governing conditions which must be present; none of which has ever been noted in closed systems using heavy brine. Under conditions of mixing relatively fresh pond or stream water with produced brine in open ponds or tanks, appreciable accumulation of organic matter (other than oil) may occur. However, even under these conducive conditions the deposit usually appears under considerable magnification to be an impalpable muck, but the solid materials (Table 6) are normally predominant. Thus, close examination of muck accumulations can be sometimes surprising.

There is no known, permissible, upper limit for organic matter in injection water, due to its variable nature and the conditions attendant to injection. Nevertheless, it is only logical to approach this problem from a preventive standpoint if possible, rather than resorting to continuous chemical treatment. As an example, a given muck of troublesome nature might be found to consist, in order, of $CaCO_3$, silt, iron oxide, and oil, totaling 90% or more, with organic matter 10% or less. It would be expected that changing conditions to prevent a large portion of the 90% solid matter and oil carryover should solve the problem. Most importantly, the additive effect of finely divided matter and the causative agents for oil emulsion would be separated from the cell material, which in turn may then be dealt with more expeditiously.

In view of the complex nature of materials found in slimes, their causes and possible effects in waterflood systems, an attempt will be made to outline the known possibilities under given conditions. Thus, operating conditions may be correlated with certain observations or reliable tests to indicate either practical field solution of the problem or need for expert investigation. It will be seen that the subject of slime or muck accumulation may be closely related to water chemistry, scale deposits, corrosion, and filtration.

Bacteria are present in all water handling systems. They may or may not become troublesome, depending on conditions optimal to their growth. A wide variety of organic and inorganic materials serve as food. Citric acid and reverted polyphosphates have been noted to cause rapid increase in bacteria populations. The range of pH and temperatures at waterfloods are ideal for the growth of bacteria. However, they do not do well in brines of over 100,000 mg/l concentration. This is a most fortunate situation, especially as regards the growth of the sulfide-producing bacteria. Recent studies at Cornell Univ. have shown that these strains grow quite slowly in the concentrated brines. Field evidence is confirmatory, such that justification of biocide treatment in brines of over 100,000 mg/l salts is rare indeed. A related fact is that control of the sulfide-producing strains almost invariably establishes control of other bacteria which might be harmful.

Plugging or Fouling Deposits

Algae generally require sunlight, and the best way to limit their growth is to exclude light. Hydrogen sulfide, oil, and brine tend to inhibit algal growth, but some strains are resistant, probably having adapted to changing conditions.

Fungi can proliferate either in open tanks or in closed systems. Again, fungi are limited by high salt concentration and have been noted to disappear as fresh supply water became salty with admixed, produced brine.

Iron bacteria and the so-called slime-formers are not corrosive themselves, but by non-uniform protection of the metal surface from oxygen they can cause oxygen concentration cells and provide an environment for the growth of corrosive bacteria.

Bacterial slime layers may form at the interface of oil blankets used for oxygen exclusion. This suggests an explanation of the emulsified, generally dirty, nature of the oil to be found in many waterflood systems.

Sulfate-reducing bacteria, or the several strains of sulfide-producing bacteria, are doubtless the most harmful of any microorganisms found in water handling equipment. These strains are anaerobic, but they also grow in water containing dissolved oxygen, where protected by scale, muck, or bacterial slime. Further, it is neither practical nor possible to kill sulfate-reducers by aerating the water in a system. In the corrosion of steel, as in the attack by H_2S, the cathode may become polarized by atomic hydrogen. These bacteria then cause depolarization by using the hydrogen, thus increasing and localizing the corrosion.

Studies by microbiologists have shown that most of the H_2S produced by these bacteria is formed under sludge or sediment, where the bacteria are attached to the metal surfaces. This is in contrast to the popular conception that the sulfide is generated while the colonies are living free in water. It follows that the SO_4-reducing bacteria detected in samples from a flowing stream may not show any correlation to free sulfide in

WATER PROBLEMS IN OIL PRODUCTION
An Operator's Manual

the water or damage by corrosion attack. In such an example, dissolved H_2S, suspended iron sulfide or black water, and nature of the pitting attack must be considered along with the presence of the corrosive bacteria.

Although the bacterial cell material of sulfate-reducers is additive to slime masses, it is mainly the corrosion product and/or the result of sulfide precipitation of dissolved iron in the water, which causes black water and its resulting accumulation and plugging troubles. Organic matter, other than oil, is difficult to observe in water, or even in deposits of muck. This material will be apparent on proper lab analysis.

However, a common error usually includes appreciable occluded oil and water. Rarely, a gelatinous, organic film may be identified on a membrane filter under the microscope. This was observed at one flood where the filtered, brackish water from a holding pond seemed quite free of turbidity. In this case the occurrence was significant because the injection formation was a very tight, shallow sand, allowing maximum injection pressure of 400 psi.

A few facts may be gleaned from the foregoing discussion which should be helpful in recognizing and avoiding the conditions attendant to plugging deposits:

1. The mere presence of bacteria in a water system does not indicate need for treatment with bactericide.
2. The occurrence of plugging deposits should be approached from several related viewpoints:
   (a) Location of the troublesome accumulation.
   (b) Nature and origin of the solid portion—chemical precipitates, corrosion products, suspended silt, etc.
   (c) Ratio of oil carryover and organic matter in the injection water.
   (d) The effect of the bacteria population.
   (e) Relationship of a,b,c,d, to all operating conditions.
3. Under prevailing, average conditions of closed systems,

using rather saline water, bacterial slime is rarely a problem of first concern.
4. Where corrosive bacteria are definitely established as a serious problem, more or less slime accumulation is usually present, promoting growth of the corrosive bacteria and to the collection of fouling materials.
5. Effective treatment of the corrosive bacteria simultaneously limits associated microorganisms.
6. Most troubles from microorganisms occur in fresh water or in mixtures of fresh water and produced brine. Earthen ponds are the worst offenders. Open tanks can be about as bad if allowed to get extremely dirty.
7. The sulfide-producers, and accompanying, less harmful strains, do not thrive in brines over 100,000 mg/l concentration. The exclusion of air is added insurance against corrosion.

REFERENCES

1. Earnest Beerstecher, Jr., Petroleum Microbiology, Elsevier Press, Inc., 1954.
2. J. M. Sharpley, Applied Petroleum Microbiology, Buckman Labs, Memphis, Tenn., 1961.
3. A. G. Ostroff, Introduction to Oilfield Water Technology, Prentice-Hall, Inc., 1965.
4. Betz Handbook of Industrial Water Conditioning, Betz Labs., Philadelphia, 1962.

7
Filtration

In the author's experience, few if any filters in waterflood service can be justified. A great many waterflood filter installations have been inspected, with the result that, more often than otherwise, the water had better injection qualities before passing through the filters. An attempt will be made to explain fully these filter malfunctions and to outline some conditions under which filtration may be advisable.

A great deal has been written on the subject of pressure filters and their operation and care. There can be no purpose served by review or summary of this material. Probably, the engineering design and specifications for installation of these oil country filters took note of available filter information. However, the design data obviously failed to heed a rather well known limitation on filters in general—that filtration, without coagulation and sedimentation, is usually an unsatisfactory method of removing suspended solids or oil. Thus, many costly pressure filters have been carefully installed in a service in which they could only fail.

It should be apparent that entrained, finely dispersed, solids and sub-microscopic oil droplets in most injection water pose a filtration problem which has no immediate or economical solution. The usual graded sand beds can only remove the larger particles. Meanwhile, the smaller particles adhere to one another and to the filter material; causing agglomeration, cementation, and eventual channeling. Also, finely dispersed oil is caused to coalesce and wet the filter bed material. Finally, the fouled filter bed makes an ideal home for the proliferation of bacteria. This fact alone constitutes proof that bactericide should be added upstream from filters.

It should be noted that dead algae, fungi, and oil are all seemingly conducive to the growth of corrosive bacteria in a fouled filter bed. After several months of filtering mixed injection water in the absence of proper cleaning and sterilization, filter beds are invariably quite black from the growth of sulfate-reducing bacteria and accumulation of iron sulfide.

These disadvantages of filtering mixed injection waters may be overcome to some extent by regular inspection of filter beds and cleaning or renewing as necessary. In the event of adherent scale, i.e., $CaCO_3$, a dangerous condition is reflected when tests show the top portion of the bed to be in the order of 5–10% acid-soluble. Similarly, if oil saturation of the bed is deeper than a few inches, the oil should be removed by steaming or replacing the oil-soaked portion of the bed.

It is well known that diatomaceous earth filtration will remove oil as well as particulate matter from waste brines. However, costs appear to be prohibitive. Removal of oil alone is generally stated to require a ratio of 2–3 parts cell material to one of oil.

In view of the fact that coagulation is a prerequisite to successful filtration through graded filter beds, some comprehensive work on coagulation of waste brine would seem to be in order. Presently, the large holding vessels and close attention required appear to make the process impractical.

Coal filters have been used for many years for the purpose of oil removal from process waters. Although crushed anthracite coal, sp.gr. 1.55, is favored over graded sand, sp.gr. 2.65, in some areas, there does not seem to be any appreciable difference in utility. Coal does appear to collect less adherent scale. However, it may become oil-wetted more quickly and it must be backwashed at a reduced rate—about ⅔ the rate used for sand. Oil is best removed by use of hot, caustic-detergent solutions. The latter facility has never been noted to be included with any waterflood filters.

With either filter medium, filter history has been much the same. After a period of use, the bed becomes cemented, channeled, or fouled so that the filter must be either bypassed or renewed. In view of the many junked filter units to be seen at the older floods, the bypassing solution is evidently the most popular.

The preceding discussion is not intended to discredit all filtration in waterflood practice—just most of it under current usage. Doubtless, the conditions existing at certain floods should indicate filtration of at least a portion of the injection water. In such event, the conditions should be properly evaluated, including possibility of near-term change in operations, and equipment selected and placed accordingly.

It should be clearly understood that neither engineering attention nor operating expense can be terminated with installation. Subsequent to installation, responsibility of filter maintenance is usually turned over to a pumper with a minimum of instruction as to operation. He "eyeballs" the filter effluent and assumes that all is well inside the filter shell. After a period of operation, 1 year or less, an inspection of the filter bed usually reveals a condition beyond economical repair. In other words, cleaning of the cemented, channeled filter bed would cost more than replacement.

The fact that a new filter bed does a good job for several months should be significant, and it follows that regular inspection of a filter bed and preventive maintenance should extend its useful life several times. Specifically, oil-soaked sand should be replaced at the top of the bed as necessary. Tendency of the bed to "grow" toward the top of the shell is a sure sign of too much adherent scale, confirmed by examination of the filter sand and prevented by sequestering agent upstream of the filter.

Filtration

On the other hand, loss of sand by attrition and too vigorous backwashing should be replaced at the top of the bed. The appearance of appreciable black deposit in the filter bed, not removed by backwashing, is cause for checking corrosive bacteria and cleaning by shock treatment at least.

In summary of filtration at waterfloods, it may be said that negative recommendations outweigh the positive:

1. Do not filter produced brine at all if good separation of oil can be achieved. Particulate matter should be corrected at the source or settled out if at all possible.
2. Do not filter supply water unless laden with silt. Supply wells initially pumping silt usually clear up with use.
3. Do not mix clear supply water with produced brine ahead of filters, even though waters are entirely compatible.
4. Do not allow fouling of filter bed to reach a point of no return. Excessive scale, iron sulfide, oil, etc. are easily visible under a reading glass.
5. Do not assume a situation of general perfection after a year or more of operation, even though the filter operation is above reproach. Check the volume tank at a bottom draw-off for black water, also water entering the injection wells.

Conditions favorable to installation and operation of filters are indicated by elimination of all the above negations.

REFERENCES

1. Eskel Nordel, Water Treatment for Industrial and Other Uses, Reinhold Pub. Co., 1951.
2. A. G. Ostroff, Introduction to Oilfield Water Technology. Prentice-Hall, Inc., 1965.
3. Betz Handbook of Industrial Water Conditioning, 6 ed., 1962. Betz Labs, Philadelphia, 1962.
4. H. K. Blanning and A. D. Rich, Boiler Feed & Boiler Water Softening, Nickerson & Collins Co., Chicago, 1935.

8

Identification of Common Problems Due to Water and Corrective Measures

The preceding 7 chapters should provide a sound basis for the recognition of all the problems commonly encountered in waterflooding and salt water disposal.

The "Checklist for Trouble Finding at Waterfloods," summarized in the Appendix, is intended only as a general guide for testing when little is known about a given problem and the attendant conditions. Understandably, non-technical field personnel are prone to refer to scale as corrosion, or vice versa if corrosion failures are not particularly troublesome. Also any large buildup of solid matter is usually termed "gyp" and its origin is equally misunderstood. Plugging deposits, being of complex composition and sometimes due to several causes, are basically more difficult to explain than most occurrences of scale and corrosion.

In any event, most seasoned field engineers, overseeing given projects, will have studied opinions regarding the main problems which account for the operating expense. Usually however, the underlying causes are not well understood and specific investigation is indicated. It follows that the "Checklist" may usually be curtailed appreciably in view of existing information. It should be noted that, in the following examples of troubles due to water, only significant tests are stated when locating source of trouble.

In accordance with the foregoing discussion, a number of

*Identification of Common Problems
Due to Water and Corrective Measures*

field examples are described to illustrate the principles previously set forth. These will be summarized, with data sufficient only to afford conclusions as to the particular problem and its solution. In this manner, the mechanism of direct and logical approach to water handling difficulties may be outlined in usable detail. The field examples will be described more or less in the same order as with scale, corrosion and plugging deposits.

EXAMPLES OF SOLID DEPOSITS (REFER TO TABLE 6)

1.1 Barium Sulfate, Gypsum, or Mixtures. So-called "hard" or "insoluble" scales

Project Description. A waterflood in Clay Co., Illinois, reported hard scale formation in mixing tank and serious plugging in all surface lines to injection wells. Much of this equipment was replaced due to inability to remove the deposits. Supply water from about 700 ft was mixed with brine from the Aux Vases, or oil producing zone, prior to injection.

Tests for Cause of Trouble. Tests showed the deposit to consist of 95% barium sulfate. Only partial analyses were available on the supply and produced waters, as follows:

Partial brine analyses, mg/l

	Supply Water	Produced Brine
SO_4	Not Present	760*
Cl	36,650	82,730
HCO_3	197	46
CO_3	nil	nil
Barium, Ba	75*	Not Present

*Incompatible compounds are shown.

These partial water analyses were adequate to point unerringly to the source of the trouble. This is an outstanding example of poor planning. If the above analyses had been available, a different supply water would have been obtained at the outset.

Field Solution. The operator was advised to discontinue the mixing of the incompatible waters and to obtain a sulfate-containing brine for mixing and injection. Calculated life of the flood was such that drilling a deeper supply well involved questionable economics. The use of sequestering agent appeared favorable by comparison. Thus, continuous treatment with a solution of blended polyphosphates, 1 lb/150 bbl, was given the supply brine as it entered the mixing tank. The treatment proved effective in preventing buildup in surface equipment. Some increase was noted in the accumulation opposite the formation in injection wells. This was probably due to removal of existing deposit in surface lines. The material caused no apparent reduction in input capacity.

Project Description. A salt water disposal system in Barton Co., Kans., had a great deal of trouble from thick scale on a Transite line. Several companies fed waste brine into this line on its way to the disposal well. The buildup was said to be worse directly downstream from one point of entry, where the waste brine was known to be from the K. C.-Lansing zone.

Tests for Cause. Analysis of the hard scale proved it to be mainly strontium sulfate, with minor amounts of barium sulfate. Water checks along the line showed typical SO_4-containing Arbuckle Lime brine to the point of entry of the K. C.-Lansing brine. Two water analyses were sufficient to pinpoint the origin of the accumulation.

Field Solution. The obvious remedy to this situation was to separate the relatively lesser amount of Ba-Sr brine from the system. The alternative, heavy treatment with sequestering agent required by the nonsulfate brine was ruled out due to high and increasing cost. Relocation of the line and disposal of the offending brine into a separate well proved to be an effective solution.

*Identification of Common Problems
Due to Water and Corrective Measures*

Brine Analyses, mg/l

	Waste Arbuckle brine, above junction	K. C.-Lansing brine, at junction with main line
Na	10,209	62,400
Ca	1,930	9,600
Mg	456	3,544
Ba	Absent	180*
SO_4	2,650*	Trace
Cl	18,335	123,400
HCO_3	336	79
CO_3	nil	nil
Total Solids	33,916	199,203

* The incompatible compounds are shown.

Project Description. A small field in Osage Co., Oklahoma, used a common tank for accumulation of waste brine before disposing of the mixture to the Arkansas River. Deposits formed in the tank and surface pipes to a thickness of 2 in. or more in a few months time. Approximately ⅔ of the brine handled daily was from the Arbuckle Lime and the remainder from the Bartlesville Sand. It became necessary, under State law, to dispose of this waste brine to the subsurface. Clearly, a single disposal well would not long serve the purpose if the waters were mixed before injection.

Tests for Necessary Data. Examination of the deposit showed it to be mainly barium sulfate, with appreciable amounts of strontium sulfate and iron oxide. Typical analyses of the brines from the two producing zones are shown.

Due to the fact that wells in this field had several casing strings, none cemented, it was found that many of the producing wells were leaking. Thus, it was necessary to check the produced brine from all wells, for the two incompatible compounds only, in order to separate effectively the unlike brines. This was accomplished, with all barium brine going to one disposal well and the sulfate brine going to another.

WATER PROBLEMS IN OIL PRODUCTION
An Operator's Manual

Brine Analyses, mg/l

	Waste Arbuckle Brine	Waste Bartlesville Brine
Na	58,400	52,000
Ca	13,910	10,790
Mg	2,182	1,807
Ba + Sr(as Ba)	Not Present	640*
SO$_4$	290*	nil
Cl	120,750	104,750
HCO$_3$	60	50
CO$_3$	nil	nil
Total Solids	195,592	170,037

* Incompatible compounds are shown.

These disposal wells were both bottomed in the Arbuckle Ls., a short distance from the edge of the field. Also, they were only 300 yards apart. No reduction in input capacity has been noted in these disposal wells in 13 years of operation. This experience serves to illustrate that, although incompatible waters may not be mixed above ground, the slight mixing which occurs when they are injected separately is usually harmless.

1.2 Gypsum Deposition

Project Description. A waterflood in Lincoln Co., Okla. used supply brine from a well completed in two or more aquifers in the Permian red beds. This supply brine was produced by deep well pump at a rate of approximately 3,000 b/d. After 25 days of operation it was necessary to pull the supply well due to a broken shaft. Buildup of scale on the shaft was obviously the cause of failure. The pump screen had a deposit 1 in. thick of pure, crystalline gypsum.

Tests to Locate Trouble. Tests showed that the deposit was composed entirely of gypsum. Analysis of the supply brine is stated.

This supply brine is clearly a mixture of waters from two or

*Identification of Common Problems
Due to Water and Corrective Measures*

Brine Analysis, mg/l

Na	46,007
Ca	6,900 (17,250 as $CaCO_3$)
Mg	1,900
SO_4	2,000 (2,960 as Na_2SO_4)
Cl	87,200 (143,880 as NaCl)
HCO_3	70
CO_3	nil
Total Solids	144,077

more zones, with the mixing taking place within the well bore. Use of an unstable mixture such as this could have been prevented by prior analysis. Use of the previously-mentioned "Stiff Index," for calculating tendency of brines to deposit gypsum, indicates that this brine should not precipitate gypsum. It follows that the trouble would not have been avoided by application of this type of calculation prior to startup. Additionally, it is worthy of note that a field service "engineer" made tests at the first signs of trouble and reported that the supply brine did not contain sulfate. Appropriate comments are given on this type of field service in the concluding chapter of this book.

Contrary to the misleading information set forth above, use of the Gypsum Solubility Curve, Chart 1, shows quite positively that the supply brine will deposit gypsum. The necessary figures for plotting are stated opposite the values for Ca, SO_4, and Cl. The point of intersection falls far to the right of the 145,000 mg/l NaCl line. In other words, chloride concentration is much too low to hold the gypsum in solution.

Field Solution. A permanent and wholly satisfactory solution to this problem of gypsum formation was arrived at by re-completing the supply well in the lowermost red bed aquifer. Brine from this zone was shown by tests prior to completion to be quite salty, with a harmless gypsum content. Finally, it was completely compatible with the heavy, produced brine such that a split system was not necessary.

Project Description. A flood in Stonewall Co., Texas, used

WATER PROBLEMS IN OIL PRODUCTION
An Operator's Manual

a supply water from a shallow well in river alluvium (see Analysis 5, Table 2). This is a typical "gyp" water and its tendency to deposit gypsum is clearly reflected by placing the values for Na_2SO_4 and $CaCO_3$ on the Gypsum Solubility Chart. Accordingly, the operator was warned that the line carrying this water to the pressure plant would experience troublesome scale. No other supply was available, and it was decided to use this water and to combat the scale as necessary when it became evident. Inspection following three months of operation showed that the scale was impeding flow in the water line. Also, the scale was hard and compact so that it would not respond to pigging.

Test Data. Analysis 5, Table 2, reflects the general nature of the supply water. The values for Na_2SO_4, $CaCO_3$ and NaCl are, respectively: 2,740, 1,465, and 1,237. Plotted on the chart, this water strongly indicates gypsum precipitation. Examination of the scale confirmed the prediction, the deposit consisting of crystalline gypsum with a small amount of carbonate and river silt.

Field Solution. It was decided to use sequestering agent at the source well and to note the effect on coupons at 3 points in the line, at 30-day intervals. Initially, a solution of hexametaphosphate was introduced continuously, down the annulus of the water well, so that the well effluent would never contain less than 10 ppm of the metaphosphate. This worked well for several months and appeared to be having a dissolving effect on the existing scale. Somewhat later, it was found that 5 ppm of blended, liquid polyphosphates would do the same job at less cost. The line has now been used for 5 years, with no more trouble from scale deposits.

1.3 Carbonate Deposits

Project Description. A line-drive flood experienced severe scale deposits in producing wells. The accumulation caused frequent pulling jobs due to trouble with subsurface equip-

Identification of Common Problems Due to Water and Corrective Measures

ment. Additionally, it became evident that solid deposits within the formation near the well bore were restricting flow to the producing wells. An entire line of producing wells had to be abandoned.

Test Data. Analysis of the scale showed it to be only carbonate. Water analyses were as follows.

Water Analyses, Hypothetical Combinations (A.P.H.A. method) mg/l

	Supply Water	Produced Brine
Calcium bicarbonate, Ca(HCO$_3$)$_2$	105	910
Magnesium bicarbonate, Mg(HCO$_3$)$_2$	18	nil
Sodium bicarbonate, NaHCO$_3$	1,857*	nil
Calcium Chloride, CaCl$_2$	nil	1,380*
Magnesium chloride, MgCl$_2$	nil	579*
Sodium sulfate, Na$_2$SO$_4$	1,092	nil
Sodium chloride, NaCl	313	48,754
Total Solids	3,385	51,623

* Incompatible compounds are shown.

The above analyses show plainly that the scale is caused, mainly in the well bore of the producing wells, by sodium bicarbonate in supply water reacting with calcium chloride in formation brine. Proof of the reaction is not found by determination of the anions, or SO$_4$, Cl, and alkalinity. Either "Palmer Values" or hypothetical combinations are required to illustrate the dissimilar waters.

Field Solution. Fortunately, the operator was able to drill a new supply well, much farther down-dip, so that the supply was salty and compatible with the formation brine. This removed the cause of the trouble and obviated costly use of down-hole scale preventive in producing wells—which at best could have constituted only a partial solution.

Description of Project. A producing well in Lea Co., N. Mex., initially flowed oil and gas. Some time after the well was placed on the pump, it was noted that heavy carbonate deposits appeared in separator and lead lines. Still later, the

WATER PROBLEMS IN OIL PRODUCTION
An Operator's Manual

2 in. tubing was found scaled so that the well could not be operated.

Tests for Cause of Scale. It was known that produced brine was heavily charged with calcium bicarbonate and that the gas had appreciable CO_2. Obviously, reduction of pressure, allowing release of CO_2, had continued toward well bottom. Under this condition, deposition of carbonate at the formation face, and even within the formation, could be confidently predicted at some future time.

Field Solution. Calculations proved that it was not economical to de-scale the tubing with acid. It was eventually reclaimed by using a special boring tool for removal of the scale. Thereafter, adherent carbonate on subsurface equipment was prevented by continuous, down-the-annulus injection of sodium hexametaphosphate. Many producing wells in this area required later acidization or frac treatments to remedy the reduced production caused by formation plugging.

2.2 Iron Sulfide Accumulation

As briefly noted in Table 6, this black coloring material may occur with all the other scales, in varying amounts, and the physical nature of the mixed products may range from compact, hard layers to soft muck. All these solid deposits must first be evaluated on the basis of major ingredients. Thereafter, the proper search for related conditions allows logical explanation and remedy. Actual examples of sulfide deposits are so numerous that if only a small portion of them were described herein, the size of this book would be doubled. It is believed that some generalities, with one extreme field example, would be most practical.

In general, iron sulfide may be expected wherever sour water is handled in steel equipment. The degree of corrosion attack and sloughing off of the product depend on many, sometimes unexplained, influences. "Black water" due to mixing sour brine with a water containing dissolved iron does not

Identification of Common Problems Due to Water and Corrective Measures

require expert investigation or interpretation. Normally, the occurrence of suspended sulfide will be slight in a system where H_2S is not indigenous to the water. This is especially true when the brine has a high salt content—100,000 mg/l or greater.

On the other hand, large amounts of suspended iron sulfide are cause for alarm where the water is relatively dilute and initially sulfide-free. The latter situation usually reflects two rather serious conditions—severe corrosion and injection well plugging. One field example will be described which shows that poor planning and inept operation can produce all the troubles known to waterfloods, although none of these troubles were inherent in either supply or produced water.

Project Description. The subject flood was located in Creek Co., Okla. The Skinner Sand, or oil zone, did not produce any brine during primary production. Supply water was furnished by a number of shallow water wells, and this water was potable, containing dissolved oxygen as produced. After several months of injecting the fresh water, oil wells began to pump some heavy, "sweet" brine. This should have been injected separately, due to corrosion induced by mixing the brine with the oxygen-containing fresh water. Nevertheless, the brine was mingled in a common tank with the supply water and the mixture filtered before injection. Trouble soon became evident from black water and oil carry-over going to injection wells.

Field men became aware that the fresh, clear supply water did not require filtration. Thus, more attention was given to clarification of the brine, with co-mingling below the filter. These minor changes failed to produce any desirable results. Quality of the composite injection water steadily deteriorated. Oil carryover and suspended, black sediment increased, such that even high and dangerous injection pressure failed to force the desired amount of water to many of the injection wells.

The most troublesome wells were backflowed into surface

pits to remove the accumulated muck. It was a usual practice to backflow in the order of 100 bbl before placing a well back on the line. Water in the pit would disappear into the sandy soil, leaving the black deposit evenly distributed over the 15 ft diameter pit bottom. This material, after drying for several days, usually averaged more than 1 in. in thickness, representing several hundred lb of plugging matter. It seems remarkable that a sand injection well, with the fill-up caused by this amount of oily muck, could take any water at all.

Test Data. Reports of the many investigations at this project became voluminous in a few years time, but the sum total of this evidence served only to confuse the operator. This result is quite understandable, since any clear statement of the main trouble, its cause and correction, was not to be found in the conflicting evidence.

In the interest of space, the pertinent relationships are summarized from a proper plant survey. Actual figures are omitted.

1. Major trouble was due to injection well plugging.

2. Plugging material was found to be mainly iron sulfide with almost equal amounts of oil, with lesser quantities of carbonate and organic matter other than oil.

3. Since both supply and produced waters were sulfide-free, the source of the sulfide was, by elimination, due to H_2S generated by corrosive bacteria and its attack on the steel equipment.

    (a) Bacteria tests showed *increased activity* of the sulfide-producing strains from mixing tank on downstream to injection wells.

    (b) The H_2S content of the water was nil before mixing, but became several ppm in composite injection water entering the wells.

    (c) The finely-divided corrosion product was "stabilized" by oil coating on the particles, thus preventing coagulation and filtration.

Identification of Common Problems Due to Water and Corrective Measures

4. Corrosion was fast becoming a close second to the plugging problem. The attack took place under discontinuous, adherent deposits to the extent that many failures were taking place on the unprotected steel injection lines. Low corrosion rates indicated by corrosion coupons, exposed 2–4 weeks, gave a false evaluation. Obviously, the coupons had insufficient time to exhibit the under-scale attack.

Finally, the sulfide pitting corrosion was accelerated by the presence of dissolved oxygen. Consistent with the chemical nature of oxygen, dissolved oxygen in the injection water was commonly 2–3 ppm at the point of mixing below the filter. However, this was reduced to 0.5–0.7 ppm at the input wells. It was not possible to determine how much oxygen was consumed in the corrosion process or the relative portion neutralized by the several reducing materials in the system.

Field Solution. In the event that the above discussion fails to bring the existing conditions into clear perspective, it might be well to state simply that the problems were insurmountable, having at best only partial solution. There can be no satisfactory or economical answer to troubles which have been allowed to reach this magnitude, especially when operation has become marginal. It was too late in the life of the flood to consider the most effective change; that of splitting the system. Only minor changes and treatment could be used in the hope of reducing the well plugging and line failures. The beneficial changes were as follows:

1. All treatment and filtration of supply water was discontinued. This water remained clear and uncontaminated.

2. Existing tanks were used to inject, alternately, the supply and produced brine.

3. The brine filters were discontinued, since they were a breeding place for bacteria and generally undesirable from the standpoint of becoming fouled with oily material. Actual tests proved that the brine had better injectivity before filtration.

4. The brine was contaminated with bacteria as produced.

Thus, it was heavily dosed with effective "quat" biocide on the way to the brine tank.

5. Injection lines were pigged to knock off scale and arrest the pitting attack.

Alternate injection of fresh water and produced brine was observed to reduce suspended material and incidence of well plugging. This was no doubt due in some measure to removal of optimum conditions for the growth of bacteria—that of the mingled waters and holding tank. Corrosion holes in injection lines continued without much reduction until pipe was replaced. This could be predicted in view of the difficulty of arresting pitting which has proceeded to the point of being well protected by corrosion product in addition to adherent scale.

The most significant results of the changes in operation were no doubt: (1) reduction in amount of material backwashed from input wells, and (2) the decrease in iron sulfide content of this backwashed material.

2.4 Soft Muck Deposits

Table 6 indicates, only in a general way, the complex nature of these soft and slimy deposits. Their full description would be tedious, also pointless from the standpoint of useful application. One outstanding field example will be given in some detail in order to emphasize the problems of open pit operation.

Project Description. The subject flood was located in Nowata Co., Oklahoma. The Bartlesville sand being flooded was relatively tight and pressure-sensitive since it was only a few hundred feet from the surface. Supply water was obtained from a well drilled to the Arbuckle Lime. This was a sour brine, containing appreciable sulfate. Produced Bartlesville brine was both sulfate and sulfide-free, with approximately 30 mg/l dissolved iron and 25 mg/l of barium. Both brines had

Identification of Common Problems Due to Water and Corrective Measures

total salt content much like sea water, or in the order of 30,000 mg/l.

At the outset it should be noted that these brines are incompatible. Thus, they should have been injected separately. Rather, the system was so designed that supply brine and produced brine entered a common, earthen pit. The mixture was pumped from this pit over an aerator tower. From the base of the tower, the aerated brine received continuous addition of coagulant as it entered the settling pits. Water from the last section of the earthen settling pit was pumped through a filter into a volume tank, to be picked up by the injection pumps. Input wells were equipped with line filters to further improve the quality of the treated water.

Regardless of the extensive treatment of the water, input well plugging was definitely troublesome. Average life of the well-head filters was one week, leading to a considerable operating cost. The pressure sand filter gave trouble, due to "cementation" by the unstable water, and all foreign matter in the filter bed turned quite black due to proliferation of corrosive bacteria. In view of the fact that the treated, composite water was saturated with dissolved oxygen, corrosion was a definite threat to bare injection tubing. It is of some interest that the addition of sodium tri-polyphosphate below the filter failed to aid in water injection. Rather, it was found that this expedient only served to increase the rate of accumulation on the well-head filters.

Field Tests. The incompatible compounds in supply water and produced brine have been noted. The initial inky black, suspended material which formed on mixing the brines was observed to become oxidized in the open pit. Much of this hydrated iron oxide, along with some carbonate, settled in the pit. The entire bottom of this earthen settling basin was covered with several inches of *black slime*, which, in turn, had a paper-thin covering of the brown oxide. This black deposit reflected the growth of anaerobic bacteria, particularly the sulfide-producing strains. Water from the earthen pit commonly also showed a plate count of 200,000 colonies of aerobic bacteria per ml.

A most important observation was that water immediately below the filter was quite clear, having turbidity of 1–3 ppm. Yet, this filtered water invariably gave a very poor membrane filter test. Examination of the membrane filter discs under the microscope showed a very thin layer of clear, gelatinous material, with only a trace of particulate matter. This seemed to offer a plausible explanation of the rapid fouling of well-head filters with so small amounts of solid matter. Constitution of the muck from the well-head filters furnished additional evidence.

Approximate Average Analysis of Slime from Wellhead Filter

Organic Matter (other than oil)	17.3%
Inert Matter*	7.9%
Calcium Carbonate	4.0%
Iron Compounds**	70.8%
Total	100.0%

* About 25% of inert matter was found to be barium sulfate.
** Iron compounds were hydrated iron oxides and iron sulfide. Amount of the latter was influenced by efficiency of biocide which was added just ahead of the filter.

The non-oily, organic content of this slime is of greatest significance. Identification of the causative microorganisms was not accomplished. Nevertheless, it was established that this organic matter had its origin in the open pits. Further, it was demonstrated that the organic slime was the worst plugging agent. Field experiment proved that the corrosive bacteria could be effectively controlled by the continuous addition of quaternary ammonium chloride compound upstream from the filter. This chemical treatment had a beneficial effect of improved filter maintenance. Also, since the chemical had

*Identification of Common Problems
Due to Water and Corrective Measures*

definite detergent qualities, it seemed to increase injectivity of the flood water to some degree. Nevertheless, this chemical treatment, or several others which were given field trial, failed to control the formation of the organic slime. Obviously, the slime could not be economically controlled so long as the earthen pits were in use.

Field Solution. For a time the flood was operated under the above conditions, using carefully controlled coagulant in the settling basin, sequestering agent and biocide ahead of filter, and a small amount of detergent-biocide just ahead of injection pumps. Appearance of black, sulfide deposit on wellhead filters was cause for increase in biocide. This expensive arrangement was terminated by the State "no pit" order.

Thereafter, only produced brine was injected at this plant. The oil-free brine was collected in a 1,200 bbl wood tank. From this point the brine received vigorous aeration and coagulant as it went to two additional wood tanks for 12 hr settling time. This treatment removed approximately 95% of the dissolved iron and left little for the filter to do. After a few months, it was possible to greatly reduce the biocide and no other chemical treatment was necessary. In the absence of the earthen pits, wellhead filter life was more than doubled and organic slime disappeared from the deposit on these filters.

A final example of soft muck accumulation deserves description because it illustrates a well-known fact that fresh water systems often give trouble which is not due to either corrosion or scale. Further, this occurrence shows that the evidence of impending trouble may not be easily recognized. Finally, this field example furnishes positive proof that the self-styled experts often fail to detect obvious signs of trouble and usually do not recommend sound, corrective methods.

Project Description. This waterflood in Stephens County, Oklahoma, used a split system due to the fact that the potable, fresh supply water and produced brine were incompatible. This fresh water, obtained from several shallow wells, caused

WATER PROBLEMS IN OIL PRODUCTION
An Operator's Manual

carbonate scale on the supply line, as well as considerable cementation of media in the filters used to remove suspended silt. This scale was prevented by continuous introduction of 6 ppm of sequestering agent at the supply wells. Also, on the advice of the chemical suppliers, 25 ppm of biocide was added continuously for the purpose of preventing any objectionable microorganisms.

After 1 year of operation, plant attendants noted a small amount of floating, black particles in the filtered supply water. This material was also noted in the filter backwash. Some plugging was noted in the injection wells, and the black slime was evident in the backflow from these wells. Two additional chemical manufacturers eagerly supplied surfactant-biocide type products for backwashing and cleaning out injection wells. Nevertheless, the situation worsened at an ever increasing rate, such that frequent cleaning of filters and injection wells became necessary. Also, duration of the cleanout effects grew shorter due to ineffective removal of the sticky, black slime.

Field Tests. Observation showed that the vigorous backwashing, while attempting to clean the filter beds, had removed most of the filter media from the shells. Remaining media was covered and penetrated by the adherent, black slime. Similar sludge was found on bottom of filtered water tanks and a sample was collected from the backflow from an injection well. Tests for sulfide-producing bacteria in the supply water stream showed the system to be badly contaminated. This is not usual, since it is known that these bacteria proliferate mainly on metal surfaces or under slime masses. Tests on the slime itself are most revealing.

The close relationship in constitution of the deposit is readily apparent. Tests for identification of the slime-forming organisms would require the services of a competent bacteriologist. However, such tests are not necessary in this case. The fact that an essential portion of the muck is composed of

Identification of Common Problems Due to Water and Corrective Measures

Chemical Analyses, Fresh Water Slime

	From top of filter bed	Backflow from injection well
Organic matter (not oil)	48%	52%
Acid-soluble:		
Calcium carbonate	12%	14%
Iron compounds (sulfide)	6%	8%
Inert residue (sand and silt)	34%	26%

organic slime, living in fresh water, is sufficient. A simple field test showed that a common household solution of chlorine disintegrated the slime instantly.

Field Solution. It is incredible that this condition had been allowed to reach such proportions because magic chemicals or methods were not required. Chlorine is one of the oldest and cheapest bactericides. It is also widely recognized as an effective remedy for most of the slime-forming organisms in fresh water.

The fresh water filters were discontinued, since ample settling time was provided for the silt in the 4 holding tanks. This change eliminated need for cleaning the filters, where a major portion of the slime had accumulated. Liquid chlorine was introduced at the supply wells in an estimated amount of 5 ppm in total supply water. This was continued until a residual of 1 ppm could be noted at all injection wells. The injection wells were then cleaned by pumping in 15–30 bbl of approximately 1% solution of hypochlorite and backflowing after 2 hr standing time. Brown color of the backflow was the criterion for complete slime destruction and oxidation of the iron compounds.

The system is slugged monthly with chlorine introduced at the supply wells until appreciable residual reaches all injection wells. All other chemical treatment, with the exception of the scale preventive, has been discontinued. Several months of trouble-free operation has resulted. Under present condi-

WATER PROBLEMS IN OIL PRODUCTION
An Operator's Manual

tions, it may be confidently predicted that no special chemicals, biocide, corrosion inhibitor, etc. will be necessary.

FIELD EXAMPLES OF CORROSION

More often than otherwise, explanations offered by field service men to explain corrosion attack are ambiguous at best and fail to provide a clear picture of causes or simple prevention. This situation is, of course, conducive to field trial of proffered chemicals which "can do no harm and may show some benefit."

A few illustrations are briefly described in the discussion of several types of corrosion. One or more of these, or similar occurrences, deserves more detailed consideration in order to render the obvious signs of corrosion more susceptible to early recognition and interpretation.

Although sulfide corrosion is usually said to be the worst of all, it is seldom, if ever, found to be the sole cause of severe corrosion. Rather, the sulfide attack is commonly found to be taking place under tubercles or scale, thus producing a pitting attack which may also be accelerated by the presence of dissolved oxygen. The under-scale pitting is easily recognized. However, differentiation between severe pitting aided by oxygen and the mild attack in the absence of oxygen requires proficient investigation of the type which can be made only by fully qualified company specialists or consultants.

The surface gathering systems of most salt water disposal projects are usually Transite, due to the unavoidable presence of air in the brines handled. Exclusion of oxygen at "closed system" waterfloods has been greatly improved in the last few years. It may be assumed that repeated emphasis on the effects of oxygen, together with observations on evident field relationships, has created a certain awareness concerning air entry on the part of operators. The use of gas seals on holding tanks has been demonstrated to be effective. Oil seals, although rather useful if carefully maintained, are somewhat less desirable.

Sulfide pitting attack on the tubing interior of a Reda-pumped supply well would constitute one example of relatively "pure" sulfide attack. Under these conditions, H_2S is indigenous to the "uncontaminated" supply water, and scaling may not be in evidence. This situation was reflected in a bare, 4 in. steel line carrying water from 3 supply wells. This new pipe began to show many leaks in 1 year after installation. Pits on the inner surface of the pipe were observed to be invariably filled with sulfide corrosion product. Thus, the anode-cathode association, and resulting acceleration of pit growth, was unmistakable. The effect of scale could not be ruled out entirely. Further studies showed incipient pits under an extremely thin carbonate layer. Under the microscope, other affected areas showed loss of the carbonate layer and continued growth of the pits.

Another field experience of rather even sulfide corrosion attack will perhaps portray the best-known example of the single effect of H_2S, unaided by apparent, modifying factors.

Project Description. A bare steel line of large diameter was carrying a rather fresh supply water to several pressure plants. After 6 months operation, pipe interior was observed to have a thin coating of soft, black material. The steel surface, under the coating, was covered with overlapping small pits. The corrosion product was easily removed by light brushing and did not remain even in the deepest of the pits. Corrosion coupons indicated this rather even metal loss to be in the order of 25 MPY.

Field Tests. Corrosion product was found to consist essentially of iron sulfide. Only a few mg/l of H_2S was natural to this water at its source. Sulfide-producing bacteria were not active in the water from this line, although a few colonies were always in evidence. Dissolved oxygen was not present at the source wells or at any sampling points along the line. Water from the source wells was from a single aquifer and entirely stable as to scale formation.

Field Solution. Treatment of the total water supply was patently impractical. An experiment, using 10 mg/l of a detergent-biocide type of chemical, indicated that the line could be cleaned, and maintained in this condition, by such continuous treatment. However, the cost of the necessary chemical was prohibitive.

It was decided to pig the line at monthly intervals and to follow the pigging process with the application of chlorine. Invariably, the pig removed a great deal of soft, black sludge. The chlorine was introduced at the source wells so that the entire length of the line was exposed to a chlorine concentration of 15 mg/l for a minimum time of 15 minutes. Maintenance of the concentration-time relationship would not have been possible in the absence of running the pig, due to the very high chlorine demand of the sludge.

After 10 years of cleaning the line by this method, "windows" at several places in the line showed that practically all of the original pipe wall thickness remained. This experience is considered to present appreciable evidence in favor of maintaining a clean surface, thus distributing the corrosion attack and preventing failures due to pitting.

OXYGEN CORROSION

As previously set forth, the effect of oxygen is more commonly noted as catalytic to other common causes. In general, there is no corrosive attack taking place in water that is immune to the oxygen effect. Recognition of this fact is doubtless the main reason for increasing popularity of closed system operation. Corrosion due solely to oxygen would necessarily proceed in the absence of other, contributing causes. Under

Identification of Common Problems
Due to Water and Corrective Measures

such conditions, the corrosion product would consist of hydrated iron oxide only, rather than admixtures of sulfide and various solid deposits.

Oxide formation on steel surfaces exposed to aerated fresh water is ordinarily quite thin and continuous. In this manner, the oxide layer forms a protective coating, and the process may be said to be self-stifling. In salt water the corrosive attack due to oxygen is markedly different. The attack is quite rapid and very uneven. The resulting rough surface is easily recognized as to cause by the presence of broad, deep pits and the partial filling of oxide in the pits. Examination of the steel surface shows that, as the product is dislodged, new, clean areas are repeatedly exposed to the vigorous reaction.

One peculiar case of trouble, due entirely to oxygen corrosion, is worthy of mention. A subsurface hydraulic pump, which produced oil and heavy, sweet brine, had too many repair jobs due to fouling deposits. Quite small accumulations of the fouling material within the very close tolerances of the pump mechanism were cause of pump failure. This deposit was determined to be magnetic iron oxide. A fine, in-line screen, placed near entrance to the power oil tubing, collected a small amount of the same material. Following these observations, a series of tests was initiated in an attempt to correlate iron and water content of the power oil.

This investigation showed a definite relationship, such that iron oxide carried by the power oil rose appreciably when water content of this oil rose above 0.1%. Again, the solid material suspended in the oil was magnetic iron oxide only. Sulfide was not present anywhere in the power oil system. In view of the fact that air is soluble (approximately 3% in 40 A.P.I. gravity crude oil), the power oil tank was suspected as the source of the oxygen. This tank was operated with an open hatch, and fluctuation of the oil level caused considerable breathing.

Atmosphere above the oil was found at times to be largely

air. The conditions attendant to oxide formation thus presented two alternative methods for reduction of the fouling deposit. Either the power oil could be treated to 0.05% water or below, or air entry could be excluded. The latter was chosen due to less initial cost and to easier operation. A gas blanket, maintained under slight pressure on the power oil tank, proved effective. It was also necessary to cease the addition of mixed oils picked up by the scavenger pump to the power oil supply.

Another occurrence of oxygen corrosion will be found more typical of waterflood and salt water disposal operations.

Project Description. A waterflood used a very salty produced brine, plus a supply brine of equal salinity, for injection by gravity alone. These brines were stable, sulfide-free, and entirely compatible. No difficulty was encountered, except that about one-half mile of new 4 in. steel pipe had to be replaced after 6 months of use. This line carried produced brine from a collecting tank and formed a "Y" with the supply line. Trouble had not occurred below the junction, where a relatively large volume of oxygen-free supply brine entered.

Field Tests. Interior of the replaced pipe exhibited the very rough, pitted condition that can only be due to oxygen corrosion. The brine collecting tank was seemingly protected by a gas blanket. A centrifugal pump was operated intermittently to take accumulated brine from this tank to join the supply brine. A pumper stated that it was not possible for this pump to suck air. Nevertheless, it was noted that the pump leaked brine around the shaft when it was down, but sucked in water when it was operating. Confirmation of the suspected oxygen entry at the centrifugal pump could not be obtained by chemical analysis. However, this was accomplished by use of a membrane sensor type oxygen cell.

This improved method for estimating oxygen in heavy brines indicated an average oxygen content of 0.5 mg/l in brine as it left the centrifugal pump. Earlier investigation,

Identification of Common Problems Due to Water and Corrective Measures

proving the corrosive effect of 0.3 mg/l oxygen in sweet brine of this nature, was sufficient to pinpoint the trouble.

Field Solution. The single, obvious remedy to the oxygen corrosion was recommended; that of proper operation of the salt water pump. This was apparently accomplished by attention to the packing around the shaft, such that no leaking took place when the pump was down. Any leaking was cause for replacement of the packing. The replaced salt water line is still in service, 4 years after the initiation of good pump maintenance.

9

Some Specifications for Injection Water

The preceding 8 chapters should provide a sound basis for consideration of injection water quality. In other words, one should not be able to visualize a perfect injection water for a given flood, or have a basis for opinion as to necessary quality control, unless he has some knowledge of water chemistry and the causes of deposits and corrosion.

There are two different periods when a thorough consideration of injection water may bring about economic benefits during the life of a flood; prior to layout and again after several months of operation. In advance of any final plans or construction, the data on producing formation should include sufficient water analyses to establish fully the nature of the brine or water to be produced. Such pertinent facts are too often found to be either neglected or forgotten in the usual diligent study of the all-important core data.

When adequate information is available on both the producing formation and its enclosed fluids, it becomes possible to interpret the data in regard to equipment required, its expected life, water treatment, and other necessary maintenance. The two periods, or project phases, will be treated separately and collectively in an attempt to set forth clearly the known and accepted specifications for injection water. Other desirable properties, enjoying less proof and acceptance, will be discussed from the standpoint of practice rather than theory.

Some Specifications for Injection Water

Choice of Injection Water. More often than otherwise, economics are said to deny any choice in supply water for waterflood projects. Nevertheless, practice has occasionally shown this premise to be in error, due to excessive costs which would not have occurred if a suitable supply water had been chosen initially. At the outset the supply water should, ideally, be closely similar in character to the formation water. This will be discussed in conjunction with certain effects often noted when break through takes place. The properties of most significance for trouble-free injection water are listed, in approximate order of importance:

1. The water for injection should not be corrosive to the water handling equipment.

2. It should not form scale under the conditions of operation.

3. It should not carry inert suspended matter, organic slime, oil, or emulsion in sufficient quantity to clog injection wells.

4. It should have calcium and magnesium salts 10% or more of total dissolved solids in the event that any swelling type clays are present in the formation to be flooded. Preferably, total dissolved salts should be 100,000 mg/l or above. This is true mainly because both slime-formers and corrosive bacteria do not do well in such medium.

5. It should be oxygen-free and maintained in this condition in a completely closed system.

6. The supply water should be entirely compatible with produced brine if mixed above ground. It will be shown later that such compatibility is desirable even though the waters are handled separately.

The above generalities should be viewed from several angles. In the event that supply water is completely compatible with produced brine, in the absence of any treatment of either, the situation is indeed fortunate. Under this condition, the waters may be mixed in a closed system above ground and handled accordingly. Most of the other requirements are

WATER PROBLEMS IN OIL PRODUCTION
An Operator's Manual

usually, although not always, native to this relationship. On the other hand, either supply water or produced water, or their mixtures, may be more often corrosive, scale-forming, conducive to slime, or otherwise objectionable. The requirements, with some of the difficulties to be expected if the properties are adverse, are treated in the order stated above.

1. Corrosion

Little need be added to the previous discussion concerning the many difficulties due to corrosion. In addition to loss of equipment and labor costs of its replacement, the products of corrosion are conducive to sludge accumulation and injection well plugging. There are a few dependable criteria for predicting corrosive tendency of water. However, absence of such recognized causes as acid gases and dissolved oxygen cannot serve as a guarantee against localized attack. This may occur due to very slight changes within the water handling system.

In the event that there is no alternative to handling sour, corrosive waters, arrangements should include all the obvious preventives. Usually, any water containing hydrogen sulfide indicates the use of lined equipment and total exclusion of air. Any saline water is corrosive to steel if appreciable dissolved oxygen is present. Trace amounts of oxygen have been observed to accelerate corrosion fifty fold in sour, dilute brine in western Texas.

2. Scaling

It is not always possible to predict scaling tendency from water analyses and mixing tests. Moreover, qualitative tendency is usually arrived at with adequate interpretation of mixing results and water analyses. This can be true, even for brines which cannot be evaluated by any known "scaling index" calculations. The necessary data are ordinarily provided by tests *on location,* compared to identical tests after some standing time. Sometimes, existing holding tanks allow appreciable time for precipitation or settling, such that slight differences in test results for scaling materials will show a definite trend through the system.

There are a number of more practical considerations, not requiring the services of an expert. If produced brine forms scale in the well bore, lead lines, separator, or heater, it should then stabilize in the brine holding tank. Essentially the same reasoning would apply to the supply water and mixtures with the produced brine. Above-ground mixing could be practiced if the mixture does not create a condition of supersaturation. Under no conditions should strongly incompatible waters be mixed with intent to coagulate, settle and filter the resulting solids. Many field examples have proved this process to be difficult to control and excessive in cost.

Probably, the worst result of scale accumulation is the pitting attack which takes place under the scale. This may occur under very thin deposits of small area, or where incipient pits set up the conditions necessary for larger ones. Tuberculation attack has been described elsewhere. The pitting attack under tubercles, caused by corrosive bacteria and accelerated by galvanic action, is much greater under thick, continuous scale deposits.

In view of the above discussion of some of the harmful effects of scale accumulation, a practical conclusion is that scale should be prevented on bare steel surfaces. In coated equipment, the main objections to scale would be obstruction to fluid flow and difficulty of removal without damage to coating.

3. Suspended Solids, Filter Tests

The subject of suspended matter in injection water has received considerable attention, quite understandably without

WATER PROBLEMS IN OIL PRODUCTION
An Operator's Manual

establishing any definite rules for given conditions. Some outstanding work was published in 1957 which set forth some effects of amount and type of suspended matter on water flow through a porous membrane filter.[1] Pressure was included in the calculation, but the possible effect of very high pressures now in use at some waterfloods was not considered. An equation was given for the slope of the curve of flow rate vs. cumulative volume.

It was observed that slope of this curve could not be related directly to water quality because the slope tends to increase throughout any test with plugging type waters. This increase in value of the slope, at any given pressure, may also be seen in any filter test where the filtered solids tend to form an impermeable cake. It is therefore difficult to select any single value as being representative. It follows quite logically that any clear relationship of slope to injectivity, in any given formation, has never been established. This probably could be accomplished with exhaustive research, followed by sufficient field tests.

Presently however, the membrane filter test serves merely as an inexact tool to characterize suspended solids, determine their amount, and hazard a guess as to injectivity. It should be added that value of the guess is improved in direct ratio to the amount of available information on the filter area in the injection wells. These considerations, while neither quantitative nor precise due to the many variables, should be of certain value in predicting, in advance of flood startup, the performance of a given water supply.

When applied to an operating flood, the membrane filter data are quite significant, but only when interpreted from practice rather than theory. Long experience with existing waterfloods has shown that definite mathematical values may not be assigned to good or unfit injection water from filter tests alone. However, when the data are evaluated from the

Some Specifications for Injection Water

standpoint of injection history and other plant performance the relationship is usually apparent and also useful.

The foregoing statements are best illustrated by certain anomalies set forth in Chart 2. It will be noted that the filter test indicates the better injection water at well "B." This water was almost entirely clear, such that the small quantity of deposit on the membrane filter precluded accurate analysis. Initial and final filter rates were appreciably greater at given pressures. On the other hand, the amount of suspended solids and rapid plugging of injection water "A" causes wonderment that the injection well took any water at all. In actual practice, the injection water at well "A" was fairly satisfactory, while that at well "B" was not.

The reasons are found in the nature of the sediment at bottom of the injection wells and the difference in injection pressures employed. The deposit became granular and porous in well "A" and it was commonly found that backwashing removed 10 ft or more of the accumulation from bottom of the well bore. Doubtless, this well would have taken no water under the pressure used at well "B."

At the latter well, pressure was critical, due to shallow depth, and tightness of the sand dictated the best possible water for injection. The analysis of the sludge, obtained by bailing an input well, shows clearly why this is not a good injection water under the conditions of operation. The combination of organic slime and unctuous hydrated iron oxides caused a relatively impermeable film with very little material. Under the microscope, this gelatinous film from 600 ml water was less than 0.002 in. thick. Compared to this, the deposit on the filter from the same volume of water at well "A" ranged from 0.010 to 0.015 in. in thickness.

The above data are believed to constitute sufficient proof that membrane filter tests alone should not be accepted as evidence for change in operation or chemical treatment. Due

Chart 2

Comparison of Membrane Filter Tests at 20 psi — Two Injection Wells in Different Waterfloods

	Injection Well A	Injection Well B.
Well Depth	2,300 ft	425 ft
Injection Pressure	1,900 psi	450 psi
Injection Formation	Sand, lenticular & variable	Sand, homogeneous & tight
Total Suspended Solids	88 ppm	3.5 ppm
Analysis of Solids (Bottom-hole deposit):		
Oil	5.3%	Nil
Organic Matter	Trace	24.0%
Iron Compounds	74.0%*	51.0%**
$CaCO_3$	16.5%	22.0%
Inert Matter	3.5%	2.5%

*Iron sulfide, granular and porous
**Hydrated iron oxides—slime

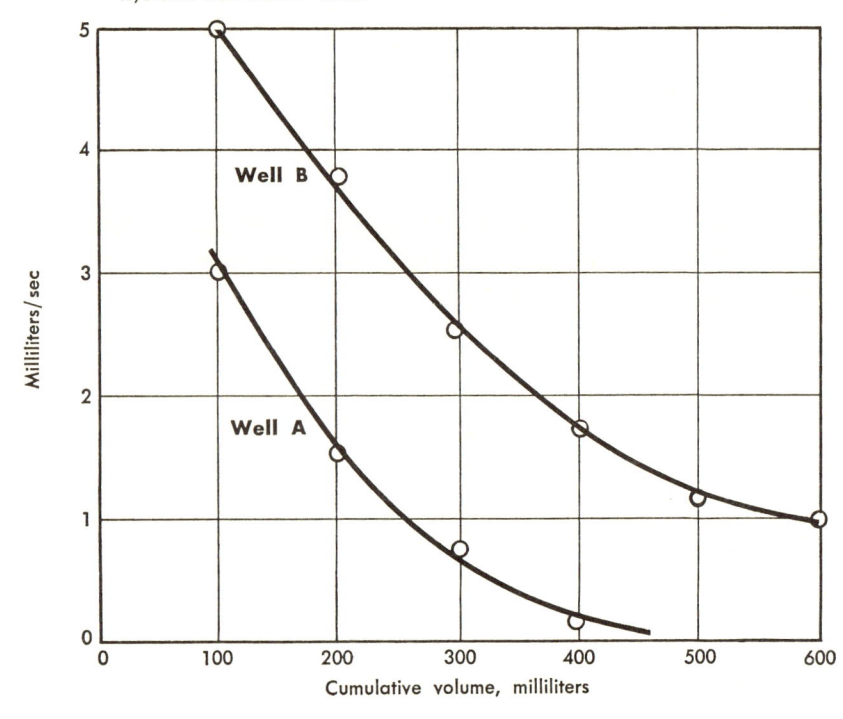

to the somewhat nebulous nature of membrane filter data and its interpretation, waterflood operators should be cautioned against making or accepting quick conclusions from filter rate or quality and quantity of filtered solids.

These data must be considered together with plugging rate in input wells and plugging material in these wells. Analysis of material from the membrane filter, if sufficient, may be used to check the constitution of accumulation from wellhead filter or, better still, from well bottom. Essentially the same reasoning applies to prediction of scaling materials. Scaling may be predicted, qualitatively if at all, from membrane filter tests and actual scale samples are much preferred.

In summary of suspended matter and injection well plugging, it may be concluded that membrane filter tests constitute a useful operating guide when the data are interpreted in view of sufficient injection history and attendant conditions.

4. Clay Swelling as a Cause of Decrease in Injectivity

The intake capacity of injection wells can sometimes be reduced due to the swelling action of certain clays which may be present in oil producing formations. The occurrence of these clays is rare since contact with average subsurface brines tends to supply the divalent cations necessary for flocculation. Clays which have a predominance of adsorbed sodium tend to be dispersed and relatively impervious. On the other hand, if the adsorbed cations are divalent calcium and magnesium, the clay will be in a more flocculated state and thus more pervious.

From this it may be seen that all clays have more or less of these replaceable cations which determines their wetting characteristics. Sodium type clays are common to the oil measures of the mid-continent area.[2] However, they are not found within permeable formations which also contain brines of high calcium and magnesium content.

WATER PROBLEMS IN OIL PRODUCTION
An Operator's Manual

The phenomenon of base exchange in clays has been known for many years. The principle is utilized in water softening and regeneration of spent zeolite filter materials and also in the treatment of soils for increasing friability. In general, the divalent ions, Ca and Mg, are more tightly adsorbed. Thus, a high concentration of Na is necessary to replace the divalent ions. Similarly, lower concentrations of the divalent ions will replace the more loosely held sodium. The ratios which govern the reaction are somewhat variable for different clays. Moreover, a general relationship exists which serves as a guarantee that swelling clays, as a class, will remain in the flocculated state, thus preventing any swelling action which might reduce permeability.

This general rule has been outlined in a most comprehensive manner in a recent publication.[3] Briefly, if 10% or more of the dissolved salts in the formation water and in the injection water are calcium and magnesium salts, a relatively fresh water will not be harmful to the permeability of clay containing formations. In other words, *secondary salinity* of injection water and native formation water should be 10% or more of total; see "Palmer Values," Tables 1–4.

This situation is indeed fortunate, and the rule is of practical value whether the core tests indicate the presence of swelling clays. Usually, the swelling type is absent, due to high Ca-Mg brine in close proximity. Also, surface fresh waters tend to be high in Ca & Mg due to natural weathering processes. The general rule of 10% ratio of Ca-Mg salts is valid more or less without regard to total concentration of dissolved solids. However, certain sand cores are said to be sensitive to sudden changes of appreciable magnitude in salinity.[3]

Observations at many waterfloods have shown that fewer operating troubles occur if the injection water is distinctly saline. This is due mainly to the fact that proliferation of slime-forming bacteria and accompanying corrosive bacteria is retarded in highly saline brine. In addition, the corrosive gases are less soluble in heavy salt water, accounting in some measure for relatively less average corrosion.

5. Oxygen in Flood Water

The effect of trace amounts of oxygen in sour brines has been discussed previously. Aside from the acceleration of corrosion, oxygen in injection water is incompatible with iron, hydrogen sulfide and possibly other compounds commonly present in formation water. Finally, oxygen promotes the growth of aerobic, slime-forming bacteria which can become extremely troublesome. Again, field practice invariably supports the use of oxygen-free water in closed systems. When only oxygen-containing supply water is available, the resulting conditions should be anticipated as fully as possible and appropriate preventive measures used in advance of serious difficulties.

6. Compatibility of Injection Water

Some requirements of compatibility have been delineated earlier in regard to the surface mixing of injection waters. Additionally, it was stated that injection water need not be entirely compatible with formation water since little mixing takes place underground. Practice has generally proved the validity of these conclusions. Nevertheless, there have been numerous cases of serious trouble in producing wells which resulted from incompatibility of injection water with formation water.

These induced conditions concerned both corrosion and scaling in producing wells. Long term use of injection water having high oxygen content has no doubt been a direct cause of serious corrosion in nearby, sour producing wells. This result is obvious, although oxygen has not been identified in the effluent from the troublesome wells. Probably a more serious and costly result can be seen in the severe scaling problem in producing wells which had no such trouble before the flooding process. This result is readily explained but difficult to predict.

When incompatibility of injection water and formation water, or "connate" water, is appreciable, serious scaling can take place in producing wells following breakthrough of injected water. The fact that this effect usually makes a very uneven pattern may be explained by a non-homogeneous or fractured condition of the producing formation, or where injected water penetrates permeable streaks and connate water is still being produced at adjoining wells. Under such condition, mixing takes place near or within the well bore, resulting in scale buildup on subsurface equipment.

Many scaling problems have been noted recently where injection water and formation water were initially compatible. In other words, the injection water can and does change appreciably in traveling through a formation, so that it becomes incompatible, or supersaturated, at the producing wells.

The condition is not easy to predict. In fact it is usually impossible due to insufficient information on effects of changes in temperature, pressure and possible catalysts on solution and precipitation of the offending materials. Induced or unnatural conditions may be visualized and described where either calcium carbonate or gypsum might be expected in producing wells.

Trouble from gypsum has been reported most frequently. Any condition of supersaturation caused by solution of reservoir rock constituents, followed by mixture or physical changes attendant to production could cause the conditions resulting in scaling at producing wells. The problem is under study where gypsum is seen to be dissolved within the formation and deposited in slow, accumulative fashion in producing wells.

Thus far, the investigation has not revealed dependable

rules for prediction or economical prevention in injection water. Hopefully, some preventive agent will be found which will prove effective at very low concentration and sufficiently stable so that it will carry through to producing wells. Presently, the only remedial methods in use consist of scale removal and downhole inhibition treatment at producing wells.

The above discussion of the compatibility requirement deserves a more concise statement. Injection water and produced brine should be completely compatible if mixed above ground. The same is true to lesser extent if mixing takes place near or within the producing well bore. In addition to complete compatibility of injected and produced waters, close similarity in other respects would be desirable in order to minimize solution and later precipitation, which can and do occur.

REFERENCES

1. Todd M. Doscher and Leon Weber, The Use of the Membrane Filter in Determining Quality of Water for Subsurface Injection. A.P.I. Drilling and Prod. Practice, 1957, pp. 169–179.
2. L. C. Case, Base-Replacement Studies of Oklahoma Shales, Amer. Assoc. Pet. Geol., vol. 17, no. 1, 1933.
3. F. O. Jones, Jr., Influence of Composition of Water on Clay Blocking of Permeability. Jour. Pet. Tech. April, 1964.

10

How to Avoid Pollution and Combat Unjust Claims

The present mushrooming popularity of the pollution subject shows immediate need for publicizing the qualitative and quantitative factors which determine oil field pollution damage. The necessary tests, with interpretation and illustration, will be set forth in detail regarding oil and salt pollution of soil and water.

The oil industry has, for many years, borne more than its fair share of the pollution stigma. Until recent more competent evaluation and allocation of pollution sources, the public and press have too often assumed that most pollution is due, either directly or indirectly, to something connected with the oil business. Actually, the oil industry probably reached earlier understanding and gave more effort toward the prevention of pollution than other comparable industries.

The occurrence of oil and saltwater pollution in the vicinity of oil wells is usually quickly apparent from visual observation; thus efforts for prevention or repair of damage come about quite naturally to protect the landowner. Nevertheless, experience has shown that misunderstandings and lawsuits have resulted from failing to file early records of freshwater quality, inability to recognize pollution at an early stage, and lack of mutually satisfactory assessment of present and future damage to land or freshwater supplies.

Any amount of oil or saltwater escape in the vicinity of oil wells or pipelines may be cause for a pollution claim. Regardless of the volume of spillage, which usually cannot be closely estimated, actual damage to surrounding land is not often determined from outward appearances. For example, the fact that vegetation is killed along a creek does not prove that it will never grow there again or that the creek will always be salty. There are several factors, to be determined by tests, which influence the degree and duration of water and soil pollution.

Consistent with the above discussion, it may be seen that explanation of pollution testing methods and significance of results should be conducive to early recognition and evaluation of pollution. This, in turn, should lead to more effective prevention and better defense against unfounded pollution claims.

Oil Spillage

The pollution of surface soil by crude oil, although unsightly and objectionable, is relatively temporary in its effects on soil and water. Some is lost by evaporation. The remaining portion is subject to oxidation and consumption by bacteria. When the latter two processes are near completion, such that only brown, hard crusts of the altered oil remain, the productivity of the soil is usually found to be improved.

In one example of record, "bottoms" escaped from an oil tank and covered approximately 1 acre of a cotton field. The field was replanted and only normal tillage used. Three seasons after the oil spillage, the cotton was much better over the 1-acre area.

Brine Contamination

Damage to soil by oil-well brines is usually of a more permanent nature. However, there are many modifying factors

WATER PROBLEMS IN OIL PRODUCTION
An Operator's Manual

which greatly influence the degree of soil pollution and the time required for recovery. Brine salinity, its constitution, and amount should be considered, together with the character of the soil as to permeability, clay colloids, soil moisture, and nature of the soil solution.

Although soil experts agree on the ill effects of too much alkaline salts and alkaline earth salts it will be shown that only the analysis of total chloride and soil moisture is necessary when evaluating soil pollution by oil-well brine.

Of the several elements or radicles present in average oil-well brines, only the chloride is unaffected by contact with the soil. Since the chloride is present essentially as sodium, calcium, and magnesium chlorides, excessive chloride is proof of brine pollution, and ratios of the cations are not significant.

The amount of soil moisture, although variable, determines the salinity of the soil solution and whether or not the soil will support plant growth. Thus, results of salt tests, or total chlorides in soil samples, should be accompanied by standard determinations for soil moisture.

When the salt content of soil is 0.5% of the soil dry weight and the moisture found to be 25%, it is seen that the salt content of the soil solution would be 2%. If the moisture were less, the salinity of the soil solution would be correspondingly greater. The roots of ordinary crop plants probably cannot tolerate concentrations of mixed salts in solution much above 1.5%. However, instances have been reported of crop plants making fair growth in soils which show by analysis as much as 0.5% of salt to dry weight of the soil and when the moisture content frequently falls as low as 15%.[1]

Nevertheless, it is believed that the salt content of soil water should not remain for long periods much above the standards set up for irrigation water. These standards are stated, following an illustration of soil tests to determine extent of damage from a line break.

Salt Tests; Soil Samples in Field Near Break in Saltwater Line

Sample	100 ft south of break in line	50 ft south of break	50 ft north of break	100 ft north of break
Per Cent Soil Moisture	14.65	13.50	14.20	12.87
Per Cent Salt (Total Cl as NaCl) to dry weight of soil	0.0056	0.445	0.385	0.0024
Parts per Million Salt (NaCl) in soil Moisture*	382	32,900	27,110	186

* Parts per Million Salt (NaCl) in Soil Water $= \dfrac{\text{Per Cent Salt in Dry Soil}}{\text{Per Cent Soil Moisture}} \times 1 \text{ Million}$

These four soil samples, bisecting the vicinity of a line break, show that the soil pollution extends less than 100 ft in each direction from the break. A fair estimate of the extent of pollution would be an area 150 ft in diameter. Some recent, dependable references are quoted on the tolerances of growing crops to saline water.

U. S. Dept. Agr. Circ. 707, 1924: "Standards for Irrigation Water"

Salt Content, ppm	Remarks
0 to 700	Excellent to good, suitable for most plants under most conditions.
700–2,000	Good to injurious, probably harmful to the more sensitive crops.
2,000 and up	Injurious to unsatisfactory, probably harmful to most crops and unsatisfactory for all but the most tolerant.

Okla. Agr. & Mech., Coll. Eng. Exper. Sta. Pub. 52, 1942: "As a general rule, under average conditions, water is suitable for irrigation in Oklahoma when it contains less salts than shown in each of the following conditions":

WATER PROBLEMS IN OIL PRODUCTION
An Operator's Manual

1. The sum of the calcium, magnesium and sodium chlorides .... 330 ppm
2. The sum of the sodium carbonate, or bicarbonate and NaCl .... 500 "
3. The sum of the calcium, magnesium and sodium sulfates ....2,000 "
4. Total Dissolved salts ....2,000 "

"The kinds of salt in solution are very important in determining the effect of water to be used for irrigation on plant growth. The most toxic are the sodium salts; in order of descending toxicity they are sodium carbonate, sodium chloride, and sodium sulfate."

Sodium carbonate, or "black alkali" water is not found in or adjacent to the oil measures in the Midcontinent area. Sodium sulfate waters are rare; a few are known in the general area of the Permian red beds where calcium sulfate, or gypsum, waters are more common. This relationship explains the emphasis which is generally placed on total chloride content, or total solids calculated as sodium chloride. A reference to various levels of total salts, with suitability to use by livestock, will complete the readily available and useful publications.

South Dakota Biochemistry Department, Agr. Exp. Sta. Circ. 111, 1954: "Soluble solids content for livestock use: 0–1,000 ppm—excellent; 1,000–5,000 ppm—good to permissible; 5,000–10,000—permissible to poor; 10,000–15,000 ppm—poor to unfit; over 15,000 ppm—unfit."

Total Chloride in Water

Pollution of freshwater sources by oil-well brines may be shown by tests for total chloride. The occurrence of sufficient dissolved iron, gypsum, etc. to cause a water to be unpalatable does not point to waste brine as a source of the pollution. The ratios of the various elements and radicles found by water analysis to one another are sometimes indicative of certain natural processes of alteration of the water. In this way, the analysis of a water in question is distinctly different from a soil analysis. For example, seepage of oil-well brines through average soil causes changes in the brine, as well as in the soil.

The subjoined tabulation shows a normal waste brine from an oil lease and the changes occurring as a result of seepage through a short column of soil. The drop in salinity was due to dilution by the soil water. The change from a predominantly sodium chloride brine to a calcium-magnesium chloride brine was caused by base exchange. The strong sodium solution displaced the alkaline earths from the soil colloids and left sodium instead. The displaced calcium and magnesium are found in the resulting, altered brine.

Changes in Salt Water Due to Seepage Through the Soil
(Analyses Stated in mg/l)

Constituent	Composite Waste Brine from oil lease	Composite Waste Brine after percolation through 26-in. column of soil from nearby field
Sodium, Na	35,324	5,350
Calcium, Ca	6,020	15,600
Magnesium, Mg	1,120	3,210
Sulfate, SO_4	105	120
Chloride, Cl	68,250	45,100
Bicarbonate, HCO_3	90	30
Carbonate, CO_3	nil	nil
Total Dissolved Solids	110,909	69,410

Definition of Brine Character (Palmer Values)

Primary Salinity	79.64%	18.24%
Secondary Salinity	20.32	81.72
Primary Alkalinity	0.00	0.00
Secondary Alkalinity	0.04	0.04
Total	100.00%	100.00%

WATER PROBLEMS IN OIL PRODUCTION
An Operator's Manual

It should be noted that tests for total chloride and moisture on this soil, after contact with the brine, indicated the soil water to closely resemble the brine following the percolation process. This relationship would naturally exist throughout the range of average water content in the soil. Evaporation and the appearance of salt crystals would cause an extremely saline soil water.

The change from "primary salinity" to "secondary salinity" in the brine represents a complete change in character, such that the brine bears only faint resemblance to the normal waste brine from the oil lease. These major changes, occurring on relatively short-time contact with the soil, are seen to illustrate the folly of attempting to prove by water or brine analysis that brine pollution came from any certain well or saltwater pit.

Other Constituents

The question often arises concerning the less-common constituents of oil-well brines and whether or not virulent poisons are present. The analyses in the above table shows only the major constituents. Very small amounts of many other elements are usually present, but none of the latter has been found to influence the toxicity of the brines to fish, vegetation or animals.

For example, a brine having 100,000 mg/l of total salts may have 100 mg/l of barium. If this brine were diluted by natural runoff to an acceptable level, say 1,000 mg/l total dissolved solids, it would then contain only 1.0 mg/l of barium. Actually, all the barium would probably be lost by contact with natural sulfates in the soil.

This leads to one of the explanations of the causes for variations found in the waters of streams, lakes, ponds, and shallow freshwater wells. The nature of all these surface waters is dependent on the terrain over which they drain. In areas where gypsum occurs in the soil overlying the Permian red beds, rainwater may dissolve appreciable gypsum on the way to streams, or reach approximate saturation in water wells bottomed in a mantle rock made up of soil and gypsum. Other freshwater wells may have unpalatable water due to the natural occurrence of excessive alkaline earth or iron salts, even though chlorides may be quite low in amount.

Records of Water Analyses

In any event, the owner of freshwater sources should, at an early date, establish the quality of the water at these sources and place the data on record for comparison in the event of any changes. Similarly, it is most important for oil operators to conduct a water quality survey of all fresh water sources adjacent to producing oil wells. Ideally, this should be done in advance of any brine production or disposal. Any changes in freshwater sources may then be determined as due either to brine pollution or natural causes.

Accidental escape of waste salt water into a fresh water body may be calculated, chloride contents being known, and the effect on the fresh water is found by the simple formula: (bbl brine × chloride) + (bbl fresh water × chloride) ÷ total bbl mixture = chloride in mixture.

Or, in the event of no information concerning the relative volumes, these may be found after establishing the chloride values.

Here is a short formula for calculating relative volumes from chloride values:

$$\frac{C - B}{A - B} \times 100 = \% \text{ of A}$$

Where:
        A = chloride of brine
        B = chloride of freshwater, and
        C = chloride content of the mixture

WATER PROBLEMS IN OIL PRODUCTION
An Operator's Manual

This may not be as academic as it appears on first glance. If, for example, a pond water had a natural chloride content of 2,000 mg/l and a polluting brine had 100,000 mg/l chloride, a mixture of 1% brine and 99% pond water would become unfit for most purposes. On the other hand, the salt would not become critical in a very fresh or potable water if only a few per cent of a less saline brine were lost to the freshwater source.

Subsequent to the initial freshwater survey in any potential oil-producing area, sufficient tests should be repeated at intervals to note any suspected leaks or seepage of oil-well brine. Attention to existing conditions and only a reasonable amount of consideration will indicate the necessary tests and preventive measures.

The value of prevention is realized when known remedial methods come up for consideration and possible use. For example, an average soil which has been subjected to long-term contact with a highly saline brine may be stated to have "recovered" only after most of the adsorbed sodium has been replaced with alkaline earths, thus becoming arable and productive. This is identical to the treatment of "black alkali" soils with ground gypsum, whereby the sodium is replaced with calcium from the gypsum.

Similar treatment, with increased freshwater irrigation, has been applied to other salty soils with some success. However, only expert testing and supervision of treatment can assure the best results. Even with the best of care, the degree of recovery in a given time does not lend itself to accurate prediction. In any event, it is not within the bounds of common sense or justice that courts of law should award full payment for land that has suffered only slight crop loss, or for temporary damage that can be shown to be corrected in a few seasons.

REFERENCES

1. C. S. Scofield, The Movement of Water in Irrigated Soils. Jour. Agri. Research, Vol. 27, No. 9, Dept. of Agriculture, 1924, pp. 635–636.
2. O. C. Magistad and J. E. Christianson, Standards for Irrigation Water. U. S. Dept. Agr. Circ. 707, 1944, pp. 8–9.
3. O. M. Smith, Okla. Agr. & Mech. Coll. Eng. Exper. Sta. Pub. 52, 1942, pp. 16–18.
4. South Dakota Biochemistry Department, Agr. Exper. Sta. Circ. 111, Nov., 1954.

11

Bimetallic or Electrical Gadgets, Radioactive Mechanisms and Other Mystic Devices for Preventing Corrosion, Scale, and Associated Problems

This general subject has been adequately covered in a number of books, technical magazines and private company reports. One editorial from July, 1960, issue of "Corrosion" is considered to be outstanding and, accordingly, is included in the Appendix.

The rather surprising and frequent appearance of certain magic devices, on trial at waterfloods and salt water disposal operations, prompts an examination of their history and current status. It is little short of amazing to find that contraptions, falling within the above general category, have been offered to industry for more than 125 years. Certain test results and discussion of scientific principles were published prior to 1900 which should have removed the devices from further, serious consideration. Personal observation during the decade following 1925 led this author to attribute the increase in number of the gadgets and their imaginative salesmen to lack of jobs during the depression years.

The survival and spread of these devices, or their successors under different names, proves error in the youthful conclusion. Presently, the existence of any of these magic cures, which "are easy to install, require no maintenance, do not wear out and are not limited as to treated fluid volume" is not to be easily explained. Perhaps, the omnipresent human trait of trying to get something for nothing is one factor. Another

Bimetallic or Electrical Gadgets, Radioactive Mechanisms, and other Mystic Devices for Preventing Corrosion and Scale

can be seen in a reply given by a field engineer to the question, "Why do you let these salesmen take up your time?" The reply was, "We need help so badly that we will listen to all suggestions."

Such condition is conducive to trial of all manner of purifiers and potions which "can do no harm and may accomplish some benefit." Cupidity and misrepresentation have been noted on the part of some people who promote these products. Usually however, the sins of the salesmen consist of questionable or unfair testimonials and suggestions for change in operation—which might effect improvement and be claimed immediately as due to the magic product.

In view of the present tolerance and field trial of these general types of mechanisms, they deserve sufficient definitive treatment so that all may be recognized quickly and judged accordingly. During this study, 20 different gadgets were reviewed as to claims and test results. Five brochures of suppliers of the more popular brands are at hand to provide an amazing amount of information on "electro-chemical neutralization," "radioactive emanations," "paramagnetic and diamagnetic forces," etc. It is indeed unfortunate that the particular products may not be designated by trade names given in the brochures.

Electrical gadgets, including bimetallic hookups of various sorts, far outnumber all other types of these magic innovations. The following outline of claims, field and laboratory tests, and final condemnation is not related in any way to legitimate electrical devices for cathodic protection. Rather, it is intended to set forth sufficient of the nebulous functions and principles usually furnished, with critical examination of the actual construction and use of these fallacious devices, so that purchase and testing of all related materials may be avoided.

One apparatus consisted of two metal electrodes in a pipe fitting, to be connected to any sort of electrical circuit. The usual claims included water softening, prevention of scale, sludge and corrosion. In explanation of the "scientific principles" involved, the inventor's literature stated that the electric forces "mollified the electrons" in the water, thus preventing any undesired results to the piping. Test of the gadget proved that it did not soften water, prevention or removal of scale did not take place and no difference could be noted on coupons where an average corrosion rate had been established.

Another device illustrates the general construction, operating benefits claimed, and basic working principles, if any, of at least 5 different manufacturers. Due to the closely similar mode of construction, utilizing two dissimilar metals which are alleged to cause a beneficial flow of current, there is no better term for these products than "bimetallic gadgets."

One or more of these has attracted unusual publicity by all the devious methods known to advertising, including lawsuits. The apparatus consists of a center core of metal of high electromotive force, mounted in a sleeve of metal of lower potential. It is of interest that the inventor stated that the composition of these metals was a closely-guarded secret, and also that these metals defied analysis. The elaborate and expensive promotion program for this magic apparatus provides some food for thought, in that a reputable supply firm became involved for a period of sales and service.

A free buffet was served to prospective users from several oil companies. Following the festive hour, the manufacturer's representative gave a convincing lecture on the subject of electromotive forces and related phenomena, quoting freely from authoritative sources. Certainly, no fault could be found with his erudite rendition of these scientific principles or their relationship to corrosion and cathodic protection. However, any connection between the working mechanism and wondrous results achieved by the gadget was indeed hazy.

The audience no doubt received no little comfort in the repeated statement that "The electromotive forces rendered the water electro-chemically neutral, so that it cannot scale

Bimetallic or Electrical Gadgets, Radioactive Mechanisms, and other Mystic Devices for Preventing Corrosion and Scale

and cannot corrode." Open discussion was facilitated by printed questions which were seen to be circulated among selected recipients. These questions received positive answers, usually in the manner of testimonials, "name on request."

No attempt will be made to list all claims made for the bimetallic type of cure-alls. The claims of particular interest to waterflood and salt water disposal operators include merely the prevention of corrosion, prevention of scale, or sludge, and its removal. An examination of basic principles indicates an attempt on the part of the promoter to apply cathodic protection to the metal surfaces by utilizing the sacrificial anode of the apparatus as a source of current.

Actually, the general construction and its method of installation prevent any appreciable current from flowing to the metal to be protected. Certainly, any such infinitesimal effect could travel only a few inches at most. It should be noted that never, in the multitude of claims made for these gadgets, has there been any claim or proof as to proper current density applied to anodic areas to halt the corrosion process.

The claim as to scale prevention or sludge accumulation would necessarily be based on the ability of the core metal to form a flocculent, coagulating substance as it corrodes. In this manner, aluminum or magnesium will corrode if coupled to lower potential copper, etc. These corrosion products are colloidal, tending to form flocs, agglomerate and settle where water is quiescent. This is an established process of clarifying turbid water. However, it is readily seen that any appreciable effect would not be present in circulating water systems. Further, if a given water system provided sufficient settling time, this would be a most inefficient way to apply coagulant which is available at a few cents per pound.

Finally, the claim that the gadget will treat water indefinitely, with no core replacement, is clearly invalid. Whether the effect is to produce current or to provide a "protective product of electrochemical reaction," the resulting attrition of metal is the same. Thus, if the gadget served its stated purpose, core replacement cost would be prohibitive.

Many laboratory and field tests of the bimetallic type apparatus have been conducted. A summary of these will serve to predict results to be expected from all similar devices.

A highly advertised device, exemplifying the bimetallic concept, was fully tested in the laboratory as to oxygen corrosion in a dilute brine. Results were the same with and without the device installed in the circulating stream. There was no difference in pH or oxygen content of the water or in the corrosion product carried in suspension. Of course, corrosion attack was identical since the water had not become "neutralized."

A closely similar apparatus came under observation due to a flood of beautiful brochures setting forth the versatility of the product. The astonishing claims were briefly as follows.

1. Reduces corrosion of metals where entrained gases are the cause thereof.
2. Reduces sucker rod pitting and breakage.
3. Reduces pitting in tubing, flow lines and tanks.
4. Removes old scale throughout the system.
5. Prevents hard scale deposits.
6. Improves clarity and general water quality.

If this were not enough to convince the prospective buyer, an actual picture in one brochure showed water molecules and scale atoms in the act of neutralizing one another. The attempt at explanation included mention of electrical energies, ultrasonic vibrations and electron acceleration. These were not illustrated, but ostensibly verified by 9 references to foreign publications.

Field trials of the gadget were carefully chosen to test any influence on both scale and corrosion. A circulating system had troublesome accumulation of carbonate type scale. Periods for necessary cleanout were well established by long experience. Operation, following installation of the recommended size of the device, showed no change whatsoever. A

Bimetallic or Electrical Gadgets, Radioactive Mechanisms, and other Mystic Devices for Preventing Corrosion and Scale

different condition was presented in a waste brine line which had a deposit of predominantly gypsum scale. It was seen that installation of the device in this line, in the specified position, had no effect toward removal or softening of existing scale.

The device was discarded after one year of use. This field test, and its ultimate failure, was cause for examination of the guarantee, furnished with initial installation. This warranty indicates full return of purchase price, within specified time limits, in the event that the customer is merely not fully satisfied. However, the fine print includes restrictive clauses as to proof of installation date, dealer's signature, etc.

During the field test outlined above, the dealer referred the customer to the salesman, who in turn referred to the dealer. Neither cared to witness or admit obvious signs of failure and both suggested changes in operation which could have affected the results. This course of action was previously noted during trial of a bimetallic apparatus in a boiler and in an engine radiator. After installation in the boiler, the salesman requested more frequent blowdown. He was informed that the extra water was not available and that, if it were, the problem would not have occurred. Similarly, the radiator installation was accompanied by a specification for monthly change of the radiator fluid. Any benefit would, of course, be immediately claimed by the seller of the instrument.

Many such apparently helpful suggestions for change in operation are cleverly designed to bring about some improvement, ever so slight, which may be cited for the sole purpose of sales promotion.

One last example of the bimetallic arrangement should be given, since it was said to be designed primarily for service in pumping oil wells. The device consisted of alternating zinc and copper plates, connected by brass spacers. Immersed in the oil well fluid, the zinc becomes the sacrificial anode. The resulting electrochemical reaction was guaranteed to reduce both corrosion and scale throughout the system. This appara-

WATER PROBLEMS IN OIL PRODUCTION
An Operator's Manual

tus was supplied in sections, and the volume of salt water produced per day determined the number of sections to be installed.

Field trial was conducted in central Kansas, where the test well experienced severe corrosion of subsurface equipment. Troublesome carbonate scale also clogged the flow line and treater. Three months of operation, with the device placed below the pump as prescribed, produced no noticeable change. Thereupon, the device was removed for inspection. It was found that all the zinc plates had disappeared.

Complaint to the dealer was countered by the firm statement that too few sections had been used. His recommendation to double the number of sections was followed and the test resumed. Exact records of corrosion on pump, rods and tubing for a 90-day period showed no difference and no change could be noted in the rate of scale accumulation. Again, inspection showed essentially all the zinc had been used up. The guarantee did not provide for recovery of purchase price in this case. It should be noted that the extensive field test was made at considerable expense to the operator, even if the device had been donated for the test. Moreover, it would be a safe guess that the operator's name was used in testimonial of the product throughout the test period.

The magic devices, other than the bimetallic type, have even fewer sound principles and records of use to commend them. Some representative innovations are briefly described.

One device consisted of a sealed glass bulb, containing a small amount of mercury. "Highly rarefied gases" were said to be present with the mercury. It was claimed that water was treated to prevent scale and corrosion by simply running the water over it, without any replacement expense. Where large volumes of water were to be treated, a number of the bulbs were recommended.

A "radioactive" gadget was found to be merely a sealed glass tube, filled with common salt and a small amount of aromatic

Bimetallic or Electrical Gadgets, Radioactive Mechanisms, and other Mystic Devices for Preventing Corrosion and Scale

oil. The principle virtue of this apparatus was said to be radiations that were set up in water passing over it, which "stabilized" the water against corrosion and scale. No trace of radioactivity could be detected by even the most sensitive instruments.

A cylindrical tank, containing an "electron emitter," constituted another magic water treater. The electrons were stated to be released, as flowing water required, such that scale and corrosion were "permanently prevented" and no replacements were necessary.

Strong, permanent magnets inserted in a plastic tube proved to be the secret of another magic device. It was claimed that "intramolecular cohesion" is destroyed when water flows through the unit. This, in turn was supposed to prevent scale, corrosion, and all other harmful results that may occur in water usage.

The descriptions of amazing inventions could be continued for many pages without touching upon all of the devices which have been offered for sale from time to time. The innovations are variable and the claims fantastic. Only the results are consistent—none of definite value. All of the above devices were subjected to extensive trial, in addition to laboratory examination. A more recent invention, claiming the application of nuclear physics to "add energy to the atoms in the water solution" was field tested by plants representing 5 different industries. No laboratory comments are available, but the plants all pronounced the invention to be worthless.

It will be seen that the number of water-treating contrivances is so great that all may not receive specific treatment here. Also, entirely new inventions are constantly being brought forth, and some of the older, discredited ones make their appearance under new names. The magic devices, other than the bimetallic type, have had relatively little promotion or testing in connection with oil field water problems. Representative examples have been given for the purpose of provid-

WATER PROBLEMS IN OIL PRODUCTION
An Operator's Manual

ing certain criteria for recognition and rejection of all the worthless gadgets. A few general admonitions should be in order.

The "engineering data" offered by the gadget salesmen may be seen to constitute pure propaganda, rather than the results of alleged research. This has never been found to contain anything but the usual jumble of mis-applied terms, ambiguous or faulty interpretation of scientific principles, and lists of foreign or unrelated references. When confronted with this confusing material, the prospective user has every right to demand authenticated tests by a reputable firm. Certainly, the costs of such practical proof would not be out of line with that of other advertising material which is freely distributed.

In summation of the foregoing discussion, and being aware of the long-standing, distinctly questionable record of the magic gadgets, a few points are listed for consideration, prior to any trial or purchase.

1. If you have no information on the device, this is probably due to lack of communication or to reluctance of users to admit failure.
2. Trial of the contrivance can never be cost-free, as commonly advertised.
3. If your company is well-known, its installation of the apparatus will be used in testimonials.
4. Recovery of purchase price is usually impractical or impossible, regardless of guarantee.

One of the several publications on this subject, by men of ability and good reputation, was observed to be more lenient than the preceding critique. In effect, it was stated that the magic devices had been known to work in a few of the many trials on record. This tolerant view is neither indicated nor shared in any way by the evidence used in this survey. Thus, in the event that a positive opinion has not been established, it should be sufficient to conclude that this writer has never observed even slight benefit resulting from the use of any of the magic devices.

12

Criteria for Choosing Qualified Services Relating to Water Problems

The petroleum industry is necessarily dependent on many types of services, and a choice of the best qualified is usually available due to the existing competition. The desirable qualifications of most services are ordinarily quickly distinguished by an overseer with a reasonable amount of experience in general production practice. However, this is not true regarding the services which relate to water problems. Due to the several causes of these problems and absence of readily apparent solutions, the correct answers may not always be prompt or positive.

This state of affairs leads naturally to experimentation and field trial of everything that might accomplish some benefit. Extreme cases of distress, or very high ratio of problems to answers, have been noted where the operator eagerly tried several different chemical treatments without any knowledge as to cause of the problems or effects of the chemicals. Of course, the different chemicals were not all purchased from the same supplier. Thus, it came about that the number of free reports and conflicting recommendations engendered a certain state of irresolution on the part of the operator. A field foreman was heard to note tersely that "We are confused."

Although this particular state of affairs may be somewhat extreme, closely similar conditions are quite common. The contributory causes of such state of confusion should be subjected to critical review. It is the purpose of the following

WATER PROBLEMS IN OIL PRODUCTION
An Operator's Manual

discussion to set forth some usable rules for recognition of sound advice and effective remedies relating to water handling problems.

At the outset, it is an obvious conclusion that anyone offering recommendations as to water treating methods and materials should show that he knows what he is talking about. Otherwise, his statement of trouble causes and suggestions for alleviation should be seriously questioned, even though his company may be one of the best in the business.

Proof of ability in the field of water problems is not to be established by any amount of apparent familiarity and discussion of other, more or less unrelated, technology. Rather, this ability can be shown only by selection and execution of pertinent tests, and by logical interpretation of these tests, to illustrate the origins of the problems at hand. Thereafter, specific methods for mitigation may be considered.

In other words, any recommendation for a given chemical application is justified only if the need is clearly shown and, further, if the chemical is a proved, economical remedy.

The foregoing remarks concerning qualified field services merely preface a situation of trial and error common to many water handling plants. In the absence of significant tests or knowledge of the principles involved, trials of suggested treatments are sometimes continued for long periods due to the fact that control tests are equally absent or without significance. In the event that a given treatment is finally found ineffective, the operator has lost the cost of the chemicals, plus all costs attendant to the delay in obtaining the correct answer to his problem.

It follows that only the most qualified advice should be sought when the need arises, also that early remedial action is to be desired. The specific qualifications are listed below which, in view of many years of observation, are found to distinguish between knowledgeable, helpful advice and that which is useless or even harmful.

Criteria for Choosing Qualified Services
Relating to Water Problems

1. Any agent for water treating materials should take sufficient time to become acquainted with the plant in question. This allows an approximate location of the trouble, in contrast to hit-or-miss tests through the system.

2. Subsequent to the preliminary survey, the agent should secure samples and conduct tests necessary to illustrate fully the origin of the problem. It should be added that only these test results and their interpretation should appear on reports. This practice eliminates the confusion, sometimes intended, which often results from trying to decipher the usual printed forms setting forth scores of "analyses" having little if any relationship to the problem.

3. Insofar as possible, the test results should be given to interested field personnel as soon as they are obtained. At the same time, the significance of the tests should be outlined orally as simply as possible. The manner in which a field survey is conducted provides the best index as to the general ability and experience of the investigator. For example, much time is saved by making initial tests downstream from a known point of trouble. Also, anyone having appreciable experience will recognize the major constituents of scale deposits after making a few simple tests on location.

4. In the event that a change in operation is indicated, rather than chemical treatment, this good news should be given immediately to the operator together with supporting evidence.

5. If chemical treatment of any kind is recommended, it should have an established reputation for a specific purpose. For example, if the trouble has been demonstrated to be corrosion then the recommended inhibitor should be a proved cure under the existing conditions of use, water quality, etc. Although there are some compounds which act both as biocides and corrosion inhibitors under certain conditions, "shotgun" treatments are ordinarily to be avoided.

6. When the trouble has been located and evaluated, the

specific remedy may be chosen on its merits. The recommendation should be accompanied by proof of efficacy and details of use. Check tests which are necessary to determine effectiveness should be provided. Unwillingness or inability to provide such tests should automatically eliminate the agent and his company from further consideration.

7. Failure of a chemical on field test should be readily admitted as soon as such result is strongly indicated. Otherwise, troubles may multiply as testing continues with increased dosage, additional "synergistic" chemicals or similar tactics often used to perpetuate sales. Similarly, the obvious success of a chemical treatment does not necessarily mean that it should be used indefinitely without modification. An example is that 20 ppm of a chemical was used in a large volume of supply water for many months before it was found that 5 ppm was sufficient.

These qualifications must be weighed against recommendations made by *anyone* for corrective treatment or changes in operation. The established service companies are continually striving to improve their services by special training of sales representatives and updating products in view of field experience. This desirable trend has progressed to the degree that service men are frequently noted to make recommendations for changes in equipment or operation, as opposed to continued use of treating chemicals.

On the other hand, many worthless products are still being promoted by men who have neither experience nor dependability. A partial explanation is that these men are untrained for technical work, and they do not maintain laboratories or conduct any kind of research. More often than otherwise, they are compensated largely by commissions. Thus, when a purchaser finally proves failure of a product, the salesman moves to other fields of endeavor.

This situation is the result of ever-present water problems and the need for practical remedies. There has been no appreciable change for over 50 years, and it must be assumed that the "itinerant" type of products and services will continue indefinitely. Here are a few examples, some quite recent, taken from actual field investigation by the author.

A. The subject flood experienced many holes in surface injection lines. These holes all took place underneath a rather thick and continuous deposit of scale. Three different corrosion inhibitors had been tried, all being increased to double dosage as recommended by the factory representatives. None of these inhibitors, made and sold by reputable companies, showed any improvement.

The holes were due to under-scale pitting by corrosive bacteria, although the injection water showed very little "contamination." It was not possible for any concentration of inhibitor to reach the affected areas under the scale. Tests proved that, in the absence of scale, neither corrosion inhibitor nor biocide were necessary. Thus, the solution consisted of scale removal, or installing new pipe, and using scale preventive.

B. A pilot flood pumped water from a shallow supply well and thence through a wellhead filter to an injection well 50 yards away. Both filter and injection well experienced considerable plugging. The offending material was assumed by an agent to be mainly silt from the shallow aquifer. Accordingly, a "surfactant-biocide" chemical was used for several months without any noticeable effect.

This plugging matter was found to be a fungus, common to closed, fresh water systems, which was naturally quite unaffected by the treatment. Intermittent application of chlorine down the annulus of the supply well accomplished the desired results.

C. A small flood had trouble from black water and injection well plugging. Injection water was slightly sour and surface lines were bare. A man who operated a chemical "manufacturing" plant at his home recommended 3 gal/day each of scale-preventive, corrosion inhibitor, and biocide. This chemical mixture, totalling 9 gal/day, was admittedly a heavy dosage for the 2,000 b/d of water handled. However, this entrepreneur explained that $15.00 per drum was saved due to local manufacture and freight saving.

Actually, it was learned that he purchased the standard compounds from major suppliers and merely diluted the products in his shop with two parts of cheap solvent to one of active chemical. Under these circumstances, the high dosage required is not at all surprising. This particular problem had a single, simple solution. The scale preventive and biocide were not necessary. A good sour oil well inhibitor, 1 gal/2,000 bbl or approximately 12 ppm, was sufficient to clear up the black water due to corrosion of the bare surface lines.

D. Another small chemical compounder and salesman displayed his field testing equipment which he employed to convince unwary clients. A so-called "gas test" consisted of a sample bottle and three dropping bottles. When repeatedly questioned as to the kind of gas, he replied "We don't know, but the test sure looks good." No comment should be necessary. Nevertheless, it is a noteworthy and curious fact that, in this enlightened age, some men can still sell on faith alone—chemicals as well as bimetallic gadgets.

These examples should be sufficient to illustrate the errors commonly made by men who are more interested in selling than in science. However, these men do not furnish all the wrong answers. Some notable blunders have been observed on the part of technical representatives of reputable laboratories and consulting firms. These are less numerous but also less forgivable. A few outstanding examples are given:

1. A consulting laboratory accepted fees for water analyses, corrosion coupons, and various field tests for 4 years. Recommendations were universally ambiguous and always accompanied by suggestions for more investigation. A qualified consultant was then employed who found on the first visit that the corrosion was due to the entry of air.

Criteria for Choosing Qualified Services
Relating to Water Problems

2. A bacteriologist was given samples of floating algae from a supply pond, with a request for remedy. His report was a delightful treatise of taxonomy on microbial flora. Although most of the strains were identified, no recommendation could be obtained from him as to ridding the nuisance. A field engineer, in desperation, used a heavy application of copper sulfate around the edges of the pond with complete success.

3. A consulting firm furnished a mobile laboratory for a 4-day survey at a waterflood. This firm was advertised to be staffed with competent, experienced engineers, who were also registered professional engineers. Their report included various water analyses, gas analyses, filtration experiments, etc. There was no definite conclusion as to the existing trouble or proposal of preventive or remedial action. More specifically, six pages of "conclusions and recommendations" contained nothing that could be translated into practical use.

It was implied, although not shown, that the sour water and corrosion were due to bacterial activity. Even this tentative conclusion proved to be erroneous. Qualified investigation, requiring one man-day, showed that produced brine had turned sour quite naturally throughout the reservoir. Thus, solution to the problem consisted of either lining all equipment or using corrosion inhibitor.

4. A waterflood used turbid lake water as a supply. Injection pressure increased to 2,000 psi and threatened to go higher. A bacteriologist naturally identified many forms of aerobic bacteria in the lake water. On the recommendation of the bacteriologist, heavy dosage of biocide was used in an attempt to lower the injection pressure. This produced no results. A qualified water chemist then proved by laboratory tests and field practice that the lake water required only flocculation and filtration before injection.

Forty years of observation in the field of water problems and related services lead to the conclusion that in the interest of sound business principles, men who are responsible for

WATER PROBLEMS IN OIL PRODUCTION
An Operator's Manual

operating procedures should use the suggested guidelines and choose the services and materials best suited to the problems at hand. These guidelines have been set forth in considerable detail, with a number of illustrative examples. Nevertheless, the ever-increasing occurrence of operating problems, having their origin in water, and their practical solutions are deserving of forceful, usable summation.

At the outset, it must be assumed that the oil producer knows what his problem is, whether scaling, corrosion, injection well plugging, etc. However, he does not understand the cause or its prevention. Obviously then, it follows that an agent recommending treatment should have two fundamental qualifications.

1. He must reflect experience and familiarity with the problem such that he can explain its cause in a factual, understandable manner to anyone.

2. With the above prerequisite, the agent may logically proceed to comparison with data from similar problems and their successful treatment. If the suggested preventive is specific against the basic causes of trouble, then and only then may a satisfactory solution be anticipated.

13
Oil-In-Water Emulsions, Causes and Treatment

Fred W. Jenkins
Tretolite Division,
Petrolite Corporation

In addition to the more conventional oil field water problems of scale formation and corrosion, increasing attention is being given to the presence of oil in water. Oil content is of concern in that it may lead to inability of surface equipment to handle the water, it may cause reduction of injectivity in disposal wells, or it may cause a potential violation of waste water discharge criteria. Oil content is also critical in some oil fields for the reason that the bulk of salable oil comes from the oil that is emulsified or dispersed in the water phase.

Water-in-oil emulsions (abbreviated w/o) occurred first historically, and consist of water emulsified into a continuous oil phase. The water is in the form of fine droplets and invisible to the unaided eye. These emulsions are adequately demulsified by chemical and electrical methods and will not be explored further in this chapter. The other type of emulsion encountered is of the oil-in-water variety (abbreviated o/w) and consists of extremely small droplets of sparsely dispersed oil in water. This emulsion is also called a "reversed emulsion," being the 'reverse' of the better known water-in-oil type.

In one field example waste brine from the water knockout appeared to be quite clear and it passed a good "millipore" filter test. Nevertheless, oil was accumulating in injection wellheads. After standing several minutes in a five gallon jug, the filtered brine turned brown due to coalesced, microscopic oil droplets.

As water and oil are produced from a formation there is a tendency for the water to become emulsified into the water-in-oil (w/o) variety until the production fluids become highly

WATER PROBLEMS IN OIL PRODUCTION
An Operator's Manual

predominant with water. At about 80-90% water cut the phases may undergo a phase inversion, with the water becoming the dispersed or emulsified phase. Both types of emulsions may be present in the produced fluids, and each may have to be handled in accordance with its own specific requirements.

The appearance of o/w emulsions usually happens as a given oil field becomes old, shows signs of decline, or produces a greatly increased volume of water. O/W emulsions become most prominent in the 1940's and are now a major problem in many fields in the United States and in other places in the world. It is the purpose of this chapter to describe the properties of these emulsions and methods of resolving them.

EMULSION FORMATION

The formation of o/w emulsions is accomplished by a variety of methods, but there are always two factors apparent:
1. Shearing action which cuts one phase into the other, and
2. Presence of an emulsifying agent that stabilized the dispersed oil droplets.

The droplet size distribution of the o/w emulsion is dependant on a number of factors in any particular system including:
1. Natural emulsifying tendency of the oil
2. Shear imposed on the fluids
3. Characteristics of the water phase

Techniques to access oil droplet size have been mentioned in the literature.* These provide a theoretical explanation for characterizing an o/w and possible ways of mitigating the problem.

Shearing action is present in the producing horizon as the water and oil move through the pores of the formation toward the well bore. At the well bore the pump used to lift the well fluids can be very instrumental in cutting the fluids into each

Oil-In-Water Emulsions, Causes and Treatment

other. Generally, rod pumps are much less offensive in this respect than the newer and higher-capacity electric driven bottom-hole turbine pumps. Turbine pumps are used with increasing frequency in older fields to produce more fluids, but are notoriously active in producing emulsions — particularily the o/w type.

Flow up the producing string can propogate and intensify o/w emulsions by further shearing action as the well fluids go around rod boxes or pass areas where scale deposition presents a severe restriction to fluid flow. Surface facilities such as turns, valves, and chokes can also have an emulsifying action, though these same surface facilities can be used to advantage by applying a proper o/w demulsification reagent and utilizing the turbulence to act as a coalescant in breaking the o/w emulsion.

The stability of an o/w emulsion is defined by the system that is handling it. When an oil field is young, the installed facilities are predominately designed for treating oil with minimal design for disposing of minor amounts of free water or water that is dehydrated out of the oil. A system that has more than minimal facilities for handling water may tolerate for sometime a starting or weakly stabilized o/w emulsion without any additional problems. However, the time arrives when there is not enough separation time for the o/w, and assistance in the form of chemical treatment must be started or else large water-handling facilities must be installed. Stability for an o/w becomes a function of the system — what may be a problem in a small system may be no problem in a system of higher capacity.

*Churchill, R. J. and Burkhardt, C. W., *Oil and Gas Journal*, p76

As fields age, the facilities to handle water become increasingly taxed, and water disposal may become a more serious problem. Increased pressure from governmental agencies for higher quality of water released to streams, rivers, and seas has created an emphasis on chemical treatment prior to re-

WATER PROBLEMS IN OIL PRODUCTION
An Operator's Manual

lease. Stricter standards on water used for injection purposes has likewise created an emphasis on higher water quality. In all respects, whether the water must be cleaned for recoverable oil values or for disposal purposes, the upsurge of water treatment has intensified and grown over the past few years.

At the point when additional treating facilities may be required, installations may be in the form of holding facilities for extended chemical treatment or equipment, such as flotation machines for mechanically separating the undesirable components from the water. Application of an o/w demulsifying agent early in a water treatment system to partially clean the water before going to a flotation cell has been particularly useful in several large-volume systems.

Materials in the water can affect the nature of the o/w emulsion in addition to certain emulsion stabilizing materials carried by the oil phase. The first such agent identified by this writer was napthenic acid, a component of nearly all crude oils. In the combined form with naturally occurring alkaline metals to produce soaps, it was found to be a very efficient substance for stabilizing o/w emulsions. Other naturally occurring substances are known to promote or intensify o/w emulsions and often these can be tied to changes of water chemistry caused by invasion of water from flank formations or from flood operations.

One noted example was the migration of waters containing barium into a producing formation that contained a sizable quantity of sulfate. These two chemicals reacted to form very small crystals of insoluble barium sulfate which, in turn, became a nucleus for an oil coating. The result was a serious o/w type of problem that was difficult to resolve. There are instances where sulfate-laden waters have invaded formation waters containing calcium and formed microcrystals of insoluble calcium sulfate which, in turn, became oil coated and a severe type of o/w problem.

Another situation in which mineral formation contributed

Oil-In-Water Emulsions, Causes and Treatment

to an o/w problem involved produced fluids from a formation in which calcium bicarbonate was in solution equilibrium with pressure. This substance, on arriving at the surface facilities, became subject to reduced pressure and altered to the much less soluble calcium carbonate. These microcrystals of calcium carbonate became oil coated and required chemical treatment to remove the oil and calcium carbonate from the water.

There are instances where iron bicarbonate under a pressure equilibrium with hydrogen sulfide presented no problems until pressure was released at surface facilities. After the pressure release, the iron promptly reacted with the sulfide ion to form the very black and voluminous iron sulfide. Iron sulfide is very easily oil-wetted and becomes a carrier of oil, resulting in an o/w type of emulsion that requires relatively heavy application of chemical to resolve.

Chemicals used in production can also create o/w problems. In "polymer floods" where high molecular weight polymers and organic surfactants are used to push a front of oil to a producing well, o/w emulsions of a very refractory type are produced. Chemical requirements to break these emulsions can be very high and into the "several hundred parts-per-million" range. There are "caustic floods" in which a solution of caustic is used to enhance recovery of oil from a formation. Any resulting o/w from a caustic flood is likely to be stabilized with soaps formed from the caustic.

Chemical treatment may be excessive, but if the pH can be brought down to the neutral or slightly acidic side, chemical usage may be drastically reduced. Carbon dioxide floods are being explored in certain fields and can promote or intensify o/w problems. Advice from an o/w chemical manufacturing company can be useful in formulating a procedure to handle these kinds of emulsions wherever they occur.

Other materials that may intensify or cause emulsions are:
1. Chemicals used to control scale formation. These are often injected down-hole and return with the produced fluids. At

proper usage levels they may intensify an o/w problem.
2. Chemicals used to control corrosion of production facilities. These materials have variable effects on an o/w problem, but many are capable of making a very refractory o/w emulsion. The use of these materials should be at the lowest amount consistent with protection from corrosion.
3. Acid treating residues resulting from acid jobs. Acid is capable of bringing into solution various metals, such as calcium and iron, which are able to intensify o/w treatment problems. It might be well to divert production temporarily as an acid job comes back.
4. Certain microbiological control chemicals can be instrumental in aggravating an o/w emulsion. Their use should be closely watched for o/w intensification.

All these chemicals deserve close scrutiny when evaluating an o/w problem, and it may be possible to modify their application so that they will exert minimal effect of the o/w problem. Mechanical improvements to a system may reduce the intensity of the o/w treating problem.

Fire and steam floods are notorious for producing very refractory o/w emulsions. Chemical demulsification requirements are usually high. Elevated temperatures at which these floods operate may be advantageously used in the chemical treatment of the o/w emulsions, as fire and steam floods may bring a large amount of asphaltic materials into the water phase which behave as solids at ambient temperatures and are more difficult to treat than when they are in the liquid state at higher temperatures. Thus, treating such a system where the heat is high enough to keep the asphalts liquified can be a great help in reducing treating costs.

TREATMENT OF O/W EMULSIONS

When an o/w problem has been identified, outside consultants or specialists can be called upon to evaluate a system and make recommendations for treatment. Manufacturers of water treating chemicals and equipment are usually staffed to conduct such tests. The service or chemical company will be able to recommend a specific reagent for the system, ad-

Oil-In-Water Emulsions, Causes and Treatment

vise the amount to use, and select the point of application. Certain mechanical changes may also be suggested so that the maximum benefit from the chemical can be achieved. The chemicals used are usually very complex and identified only with a trade name and number. Most often these reagents will be called polyelectrolytes and largely available as liquids which can be pumped directly into the fluid stream in very small but continuous amounts.

O/W emulsions are ordinarily very dilute; that is, there is often not much oil involved. Concentrations below 1000 ppm are most commonly encountered. Any treatment plan must take into consideration that the emulsified oil droplets must be brought together somehow and in the presence of the proper chemical.

Movement of the well fluids through surface flowlines is usually accompanied with a turbulent flow which we can simply call agitation. After a chemical has been applied to an o/w emulsion, flowline turbulence or agitation is useful in bringing the chemicalized oil droplets together so that they can coalesce and grow to a larger size for settling. Some chemical demulsification reagents require severe and lengthy agitation while others do not need as much.

Some chemicals react quickly and do not require extended agitation. Other chemicals may improve greatly as agitation is extended. In any event, it is usually preferred to inject the o/w demulsifier somewhere along the flowline or at a manifold so that by the time the fluids reach a knockout, gun barrel, wash tank, or settling basin, the emulsion has been broken by the appropriate agitation, and the o/w is now ready for the necessary quiescence to separate the two phases.

Occasionally it may be necessary to treat the water-in-oil emulsion first and then treat the gathered o/w emulsion subsequently. This may be the preferred procedure if the system is producing a relatively large amount of w/o emulsion in which the water emulsified into the oil may itself be an o/w emulsion.

WATER PROBLEMS IN OIL PRODUCTION
An Operator's Manual

WATER TREATING SYSTEMS, SCHEMATIC

Four typical water treating systems are illustrated here. (Refer to Chart 3, drawings of water-treating systems.)

Application of heat to assist the breaking of an o/w emulsion is not as important as in the dehydration of w/o emulsions, though if heat is an integral part of the treating system, it would be preferable to use it. Generally if the oil phase is a liquid at the temperature of production, the addition of heat will not be needed. But if the produced fluids are from a steam or fire flood, there may be present portions of asphaltic or waxy substances that behave as solids at atmospheric temperatures. In this case heat may be very helpful to o/w demulsification.

There are other aids to demulsification that may be helpful. Corrugated plate interceptors have been applied in some instances to contact the broken emulsion and remove it from the water. These interceptors occupy very little space as compared to typical settling ponds. In-line mixers have been useful in shortening agitation requirements. Cascading steps have been used in oil fields where more agitation was required to, break the o/w emulstion. Cascading steps are seldom used now.

EVALUATION OF O/W TREATMENT, ANALYTICAL SURVEYS

A critical aspect of any o/w treating program is the analytical determination of the oil content of the water at various points in the system. If the system is apparently handling the o/w problem, the question arises as to how well the system is functioning. Ordinarily a laboratory will conduct an extraction, weigh the recovered oil, and report the result as "ppm oil" or "milligrams oil per liter." Both values are nearly like and, indeed, are often used interchangeably.

Newer methods, and particularly those approved by various governmental agencies, involve extraction with a fluorocar-

Schematic Water Treating Systems
Chart 3

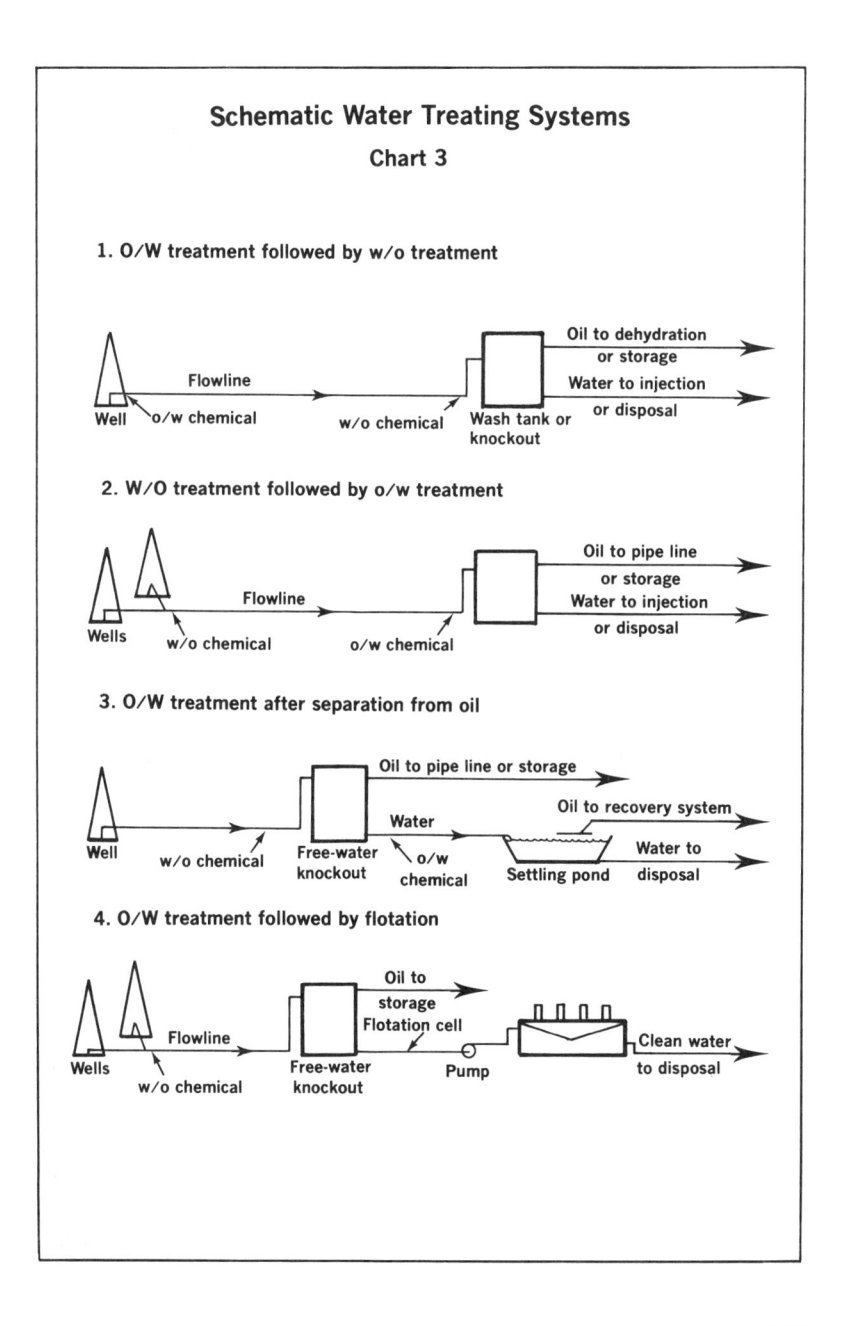

1. O/W treatment followed by w/o treatment

Well — o/w chemical — Flowline — w/o chemical — Wash tank or knockout — Oil to dehydration or storage / Water to injection or disposal

2. W/O treatment followed by o/w treatment

Wells — w/o chemical — Flowline — o/w chemical — Oil to pipe line or storage / Water to injection or disposal

3. O/W treatment after separation from oil

Well — w/o chemical — Free-water knockout — Oil to pipe line or storage / Water — o/w chemical — Settling pond — Oil to recovery system / Water to disposal

4. O/W treatment followed by flotation

Wells — w/o chemical — Flowline — Free-water knockout — Oil to storage / Flotation cell — Pump — Clean water to disposal

WATER PROBLEMS IN OIL PRODUCTION
An Operator's Manual

bon solvent and measurement of the extracted oil by means of an infra-red spectrophotometer set at 3.37 microns wavelength.[1] This is an expensive piece of equipment and not generally a part of smaller laboratories. It may be necessary to find a laboratory that can do this kind of analysis if governmental regulations are involved. If the waters treated are not subject to environmental regulations, but need to be quantitatively evaluated, there are a number of colorimetric procedures that can be used.

Two examples of o/w treatment by settling are tabulated:

Kern River Field
California
Example 1: Untreated Stream   480 ppm oil
            Chemical[2] Treatment Rate   10 ppm
            Final Effluent Stream   5 ppm oil

1. Methods for Chemical Analysis of Water and Waste, 1974. Methods Development and Quality Assurance Reserch Laboratory, National Environmental Research Center, Cincinnatti, Ohio 45268. Also known as STORET 00560 Method.
2. Tretolite Demulsifier J-162.

Example 2: Untreated Stream   600+ ppm oil
            Chemical[3] Treatment Rate   12   ppm
            Final Effluent Stream   6   ppm
NOTE: The water from Example 2 was further clarified by putting it through a flotation cell. At the discharge of the machine the oil content was less than 1 ppm.

Water analysis for non-oily components can be useful in understanding o/w problems. An increase in hardness (calcium and magnesium) may be an indicator that water quality is changing and that any o/w problem present may also change and require that chemical treatment be changed. A general decrease or increase in dissolved solids content could indicate a breakthrough of outside waters into the producing horizon. Increase of iron or hydrogen sulfide may suggest that black water is an approaching problem. An increase of iron may also indicate that corrosion control has been lost which may, in turn, affect the o/w problem. pH measurements are valuable in following the return of an acid job which, as has been mentioned earlier, can intensify o/w problems greatly. Water analyses are an important part of the general understanding of water problems and may aid materially in explaining changes in water treatment.

FLOTATION

Flotation is a process in which a gas is used in a mechanical system to give a lift or buoyancy to suspended oil or solids. It is, then, the opposite of sedimentation. The first type of flotation discussed is dissolved-air flotation which involves contacting the water in a pressurized chamber with air or gas. The gas dissolves into the water, previously chemicalized, in direct proportion to the pressure applied. Pressures commonly encountered are of the order of 50 to 90 pounds guage.

After the water has been saturated with gas, the water is conducted to the flotation chamber through a pressure reducing valve. The water, now at atmospheric pressure, loses the supersaturated portion of the gas in the form of very small bubbles. These bubbles attach themselves to a chemicalized oil or solid particle, grow in size, and rise to the top of the flotation cell, where they are removed by rotating skimmer into a launderer for removal. The water remaining in the cell is usually quite clean and adaptable to whatever process it must serve, whether for injection or disposal to surface facilities.

Actually, there are three principal variations of dissolved-air flotation. These are "Full-Flow Operation", "Split-Flow Operation", and "Recycle Operation." Chart 4 shows brief schematics of the three. Full-flow operation consists of dissolving gas into the entire stream and allowing release at the flotation cell, Chart 5. This action provides maximum gas solution and maximum bubble formation, which provides the best chance to contact the dispersed particles.

In the Split-Flow operation only part of the incoming stream is pressurized, while the remainder of the stream continues

WATER PROBLEMS IN OIL PRODUCTION
An Operator's Manual

Flotation Systems

Chart 4

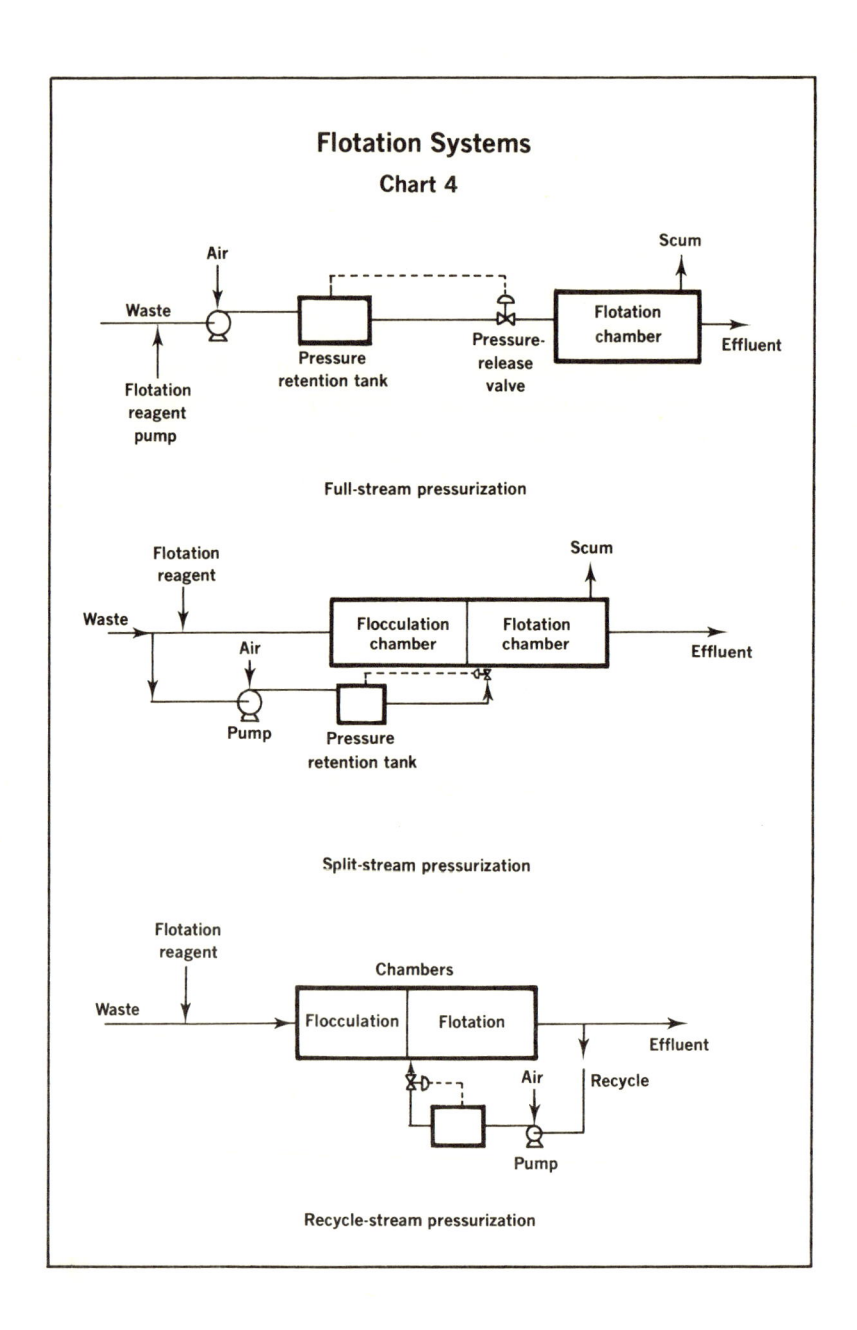

Full-stream pressurization

Split-stream pressurization

Recycle-stream pressurization

Oil-In-Water Emulsions, Causes and Treatment

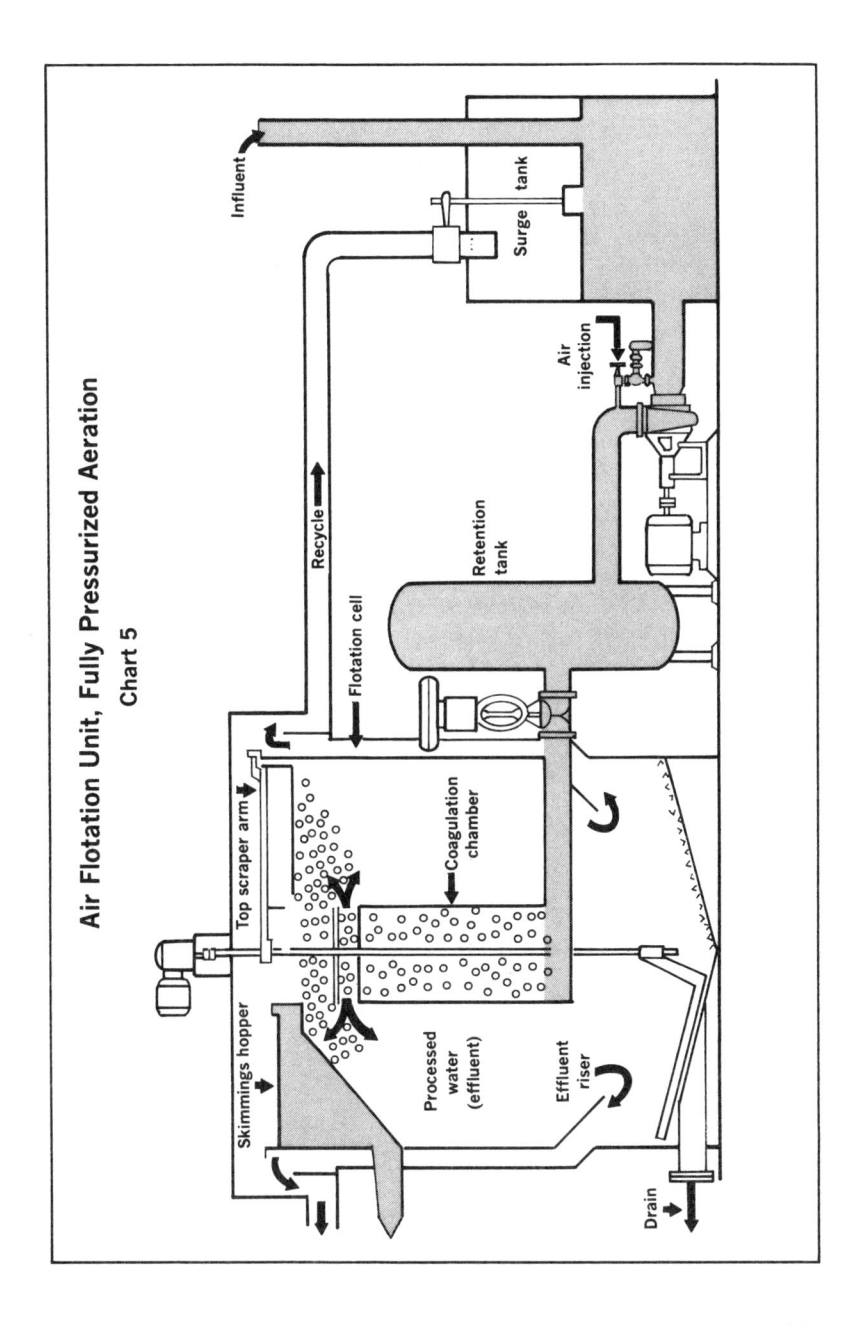

Air Flotation Unit, Fully Pressurized Aeration
Chart 5

WATER PROBLEMS IN OIL PRODUCTION
An Operator's Manual

directly to the flotation chamber. At the flotation chamber the streams comingle, and the flotation process takes place. There is less gas used in this process, which may make the process slightly less effective than the Full-Flow flotation.

In the Recycle Operation, Chart 6, gas is pressurized in a portion of the cleaned water which is then recycled back to the flotation chamber, where it comingles with the chemicalized incoming stream. The flotation process then takes place in a manner similar to the above applications. The chief advantage of this system is that the cleaned water has little or no demand for the dissolved gas, which can be transferred entirely to the incoming stream for flotation.

The dissolved-air flotation processes have been used for a number of years up to now with varying success. There is now a newer type of flotation rapidly coming into use called the Induced Air Flotation process, Chart 7. In this application air is induced into the water by a rapidly rotating impeller. This impeller is so placed in the flotation cell that in its normal operation it draws in gas from above and water from below and ejects the mixture sideways with such a turbulent action that the air is broken up into a myriad of very small bubbles. These bubbles attach themselves to chemicalized oil or solid particles and lift them quickly to the surface.

It is necessary for the water to be chemicalized with the proper flotation reagent before entering the machine. To prevent the water from spinning with the impeller, a perforated stator is placed close to the rotor. This acts to stop any rotation tendency of the water and also aids in the separation of the bubbles to the surface. At the top of the cell the bubbles become an oily froth which is swept off by a system of skimmer paddles and aprons. These induced air machines pull in many times more air or gas than the dissolved air process, which makes them a more efficient process than the dissolved air processes.

The efficiency of the "Depurator"* induced air flotation machine can be seen in the following examples.

Oil-In-Water Emulsions, Causes and Treatment

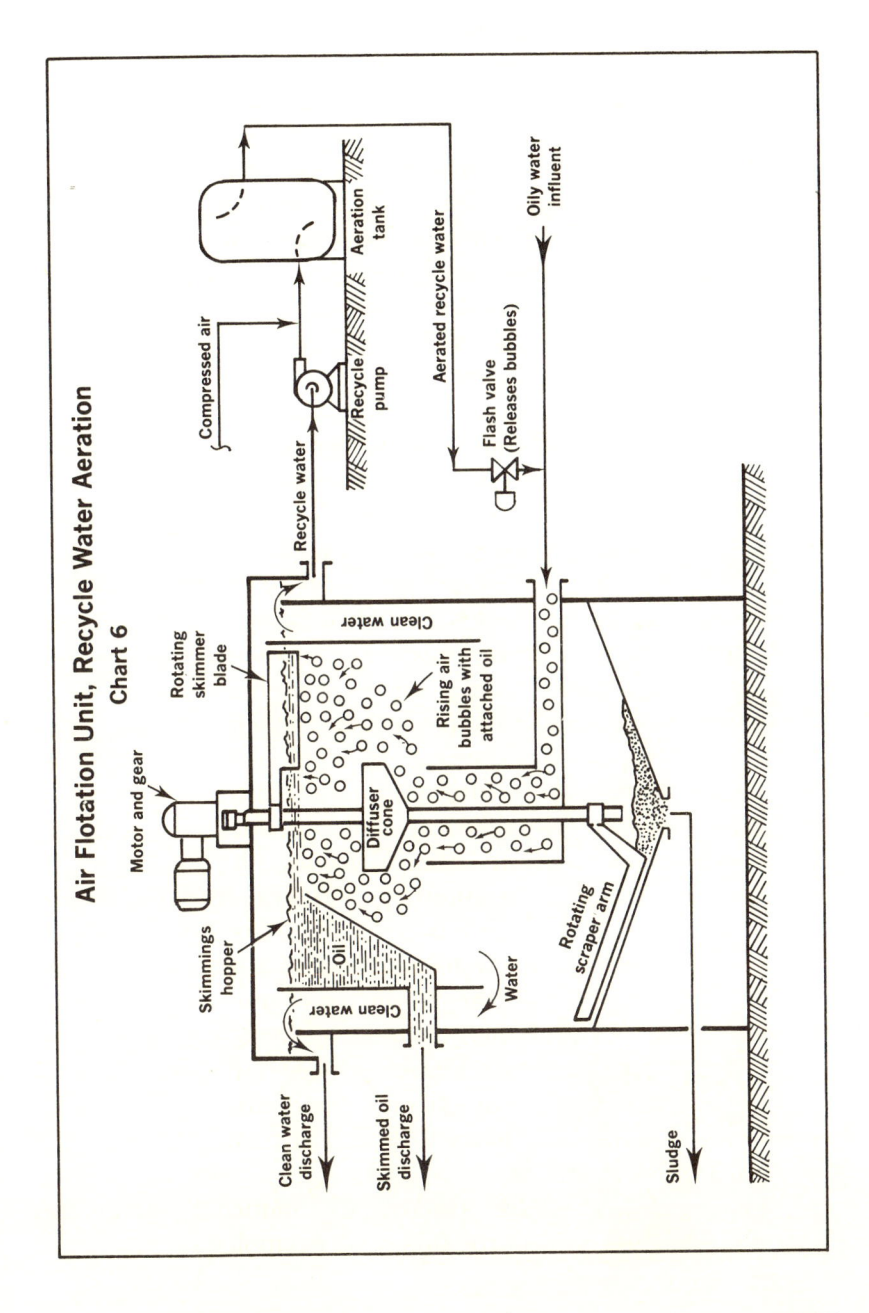

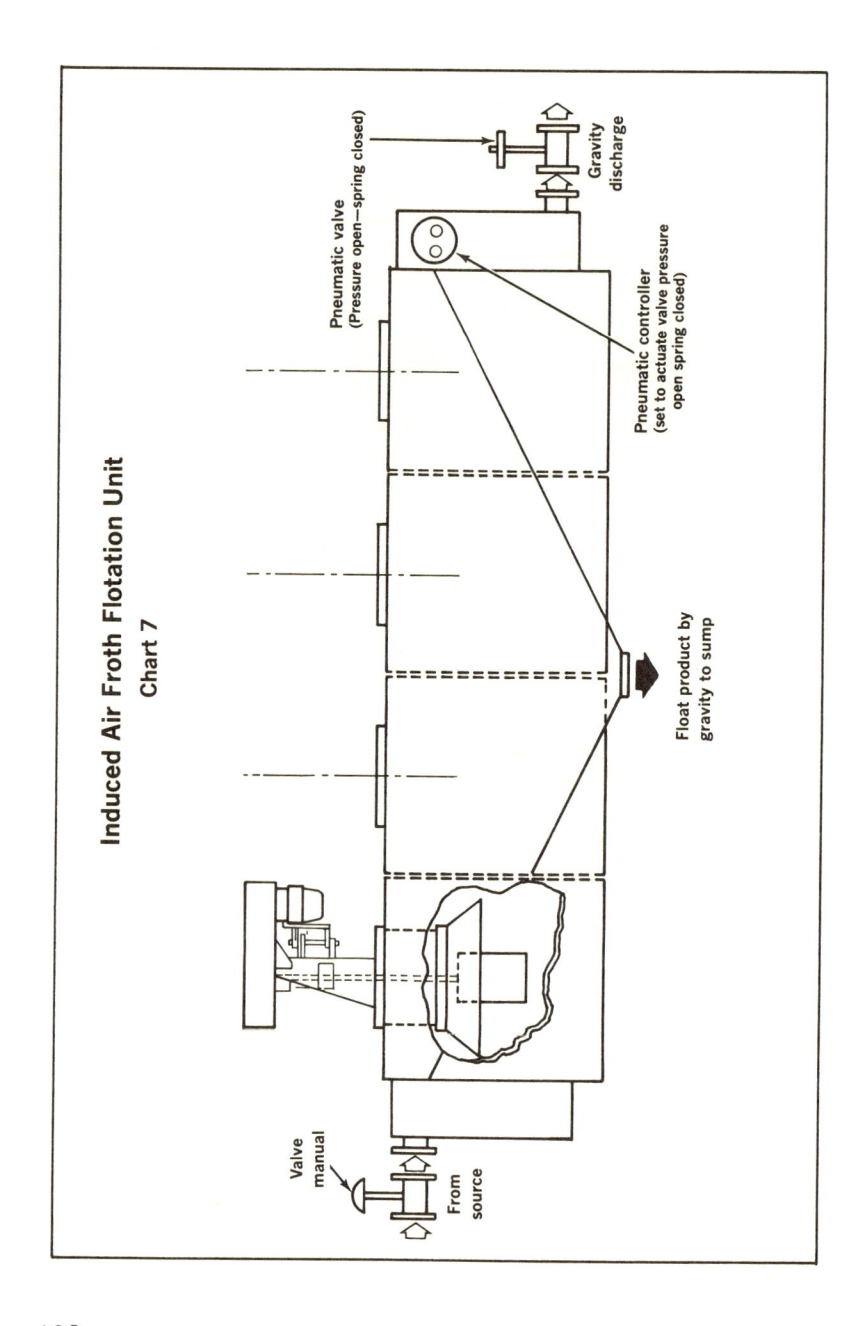

WATER PROBLEMS IN OIL PRODUCTION
An Operator's Manual

Induced Air Froth Flotation Unit
Chart 7

- Gravity discharge
- Pneumatic valve (Pressure open—spring closed)
- Pneumatic controller (set to actuate valve pressure open spring closed)
- Float product by gravity to sump
- Valve manual
- From source

138

Oil-In-Water Emulsions, Causes and Treatment

Example 1: 150 ppm oil on untreated stream
26 ppm oil after Depurator,
5 parts flotation chemical[1]
18 ppm oil after Depurator,
5 parts flotation chemical[1]
10 ppm oil after Depurator,
10 parts flotation chemical[1]

3. Tretolite Demulsifier J-162.
*Product of Envirotech, Wemco Division, Sacramento, CA.
1. Tretolite Flotation Reagent FR-52.
2. Tretolite o/w Demulsifier J.172.
3. Tretolite Flotation Reagent FR-67.

Efficiency of induced air flotation machines is of the order of 90-95%, and though these machines are often subjected to higher contaminant levels, their efficiency stays at the same level. These machines, as well as the dissolved air machines, do lose efficiency as the contamination levels reach the 1500-2000 ppm oil mark, and may fail completely if sizable amounts of free oil come through. The free oil acts to break the foam into oil and water which, of course, destroys the flotation action. Other examples of results from oil field application of a "Depurator" are:

Salt Creek, WY. Influent, 80 ppm oil. Effluent, 8 ppm oil, with 2.5 ppm chemical.[2]
Salt Creek, WY. Influent, 132 ppm oil. Effluent, 4 ppm oil, with 4 ppm chemical.[2]
Salt Creek, WY. Influent, 75 ppm oil. Effluent, 5 ppm oil, with 4 ppm chemical.[3]

The physical makeup of induced air flotation machines, of which the Depurator is one example, consists of 4 or more cells in series. Cascading the water through these several cells contributes greatly to the increased efficiency of the unit. Induced air flotation machines range in capacities from 150 gallons per minute (5,140 barrels/day) to over 4000 gallons per minute (137,000 barrels/day). These machines are fabricated so that they can be closed and operated in the absence of air and in the presence of some other gas. There are many instances where air can cause oxidation problems, and with these machines closed an inert gas is used for the aeration function. A typical inert gas is field gas from oil field sources.

Examples of air and oxidation complications are:
1. Sulfur oxidized to the collodial state when hydrogen sulfide laden waters are subjected to flotation.
2. Oxidation of soluble ferrous iron to the insoluble ferric iron, which manifests itself often as a voluminous red floc entrained in the water. Application of a different type of flotation reagent may be necessary if iron is a problem.

There may also be occasions where it is desirable to keep the cells covered so that offensive gasses or odors are not emitted to the atmosphere. On the other hand, it has been found that gas displacement can be useful. Certain waters that must be enriched with oxygen before disposal to certain streams or bodies of water can be treated in such a manner with an induced air flotation machine. This treatment can bring up the oxygen content of the water to the point where it will not endanger wildlife that is present in the receiving waters.

Thus induced air flotation not only offers technology to clean suspended solids and solids out of the water, but a method whereby gasses can be removed from water.

Before a flotation cell can be recommended for a certain application, carefully monitored laboratory tests should be carried out. There are laboratory sized flotation cells available for bench testing, and often the vendors of the flotation cells or chemical flotation reagents can conduct such tests and make a recommendation for proper flotation cell size and preferred chemical. As in the case of settling, chemicals are usually necessary for the proper operation of the flotation cell. These chemicals are often the same as those used for o/w demulsification and appear to act as a briding agent between the dispersed particle and the entrained gas.

Flotation offers maximum cleaning ability with minimum space requirements. In this respect flotation cells and Depurators are ideally suited for off-shore installations on production platforms. Here they are ideally suited for cleaning water before it is discharged to the ocean. The future of flotation appears very secure for the cleaning of oilfield waters, petroleum refinery waters, and even industrial effluent waters.

REFERENCES

1. R. J. Churchill, and C. W. Burkhardt, The Oil and Gas Journal, p. 76, June 14, 1976.
2. M. de Groote, The Science of Petroleum, 1:11, 618, 1938.
3. J. J. Brunsmonn and J. Cornelissen, JWPCF 51, p. 44, 1962.

Appendix

Reference Tables and Information Commonly Used in Oil Field Water Problems.

Well Leaks as Indicated by Water Analysis

Any appearance of water foreign to the oil zone in producing oil wells doubtless belongs in the category of water problems in oil production. However, the subject is not considered to merit a full chapter in this book. The following summary sets forth the importance of water analysis as applied to well leaks and related problems.

The first water appearing with produced oil should be given a complete analysis, for the following reasons:

1. The water may not be from the producing formation. If it is not, then re-cementing or other workover may save the well.
2. In the event that the analysis proves the water to be from the oil zone, then it should be placed on record for reference and various uses. For example, both corrosive water and scale-forming water require special equipment and facilities for treating. These and other characteristics must be considered when re-injecting produced brine.

Entry of foreign water in producing wells may be indicated by one or more existing conditions, such as sharp rise in volume of produced water, the appearance of muddy water, unusual scale on tubing or rods, or a change in specific gravity or other properties of the water produced with the oil. Usually, a study of current well conditions and well history gives some idea as to the source of the leak. It may be necessary to compare the water to that in nearby wells. It is very important to consider all the available information.

Water foreign to the oil zone may sometimes be identified

Appendix

by simple tests or partial analyses. More often, more complete analyses are required, to compare with initial produced water or water from nearby wells. In any event, both analysis and interpretation should be made by "one skilled in the art." Tests made with inferior field equipment are subject to error, as well as the interpretation usually furnished with such tests. Reputable laboratories employ chemists having considerable experience in all phases of water chemistry. In addition, these laboratories usually have a file of subsurface water analyses for comparison and location of leaks.

Appendix

Check List for Trouble Finding at Waterfloods

A. Descriptive (general summary of system)
   1. *Supply water:* Well depth, formation, amount pumped, type pump and operation. Pond, lake or stream; any pertinent conditions.
   2. *Holding basins:* Size, material, open or closed. Deposits or corrosion?
   3. *Filters:* Type and operation. Kind of filter media. Inspect for fouling or cementation if used more than one year.
   4. *Injection pumps and lines:* Injection pressure and history. Coated lines? Corrosion or scale?
   5. *Injection wells:* Injection formation, name and general information as to perm., plugging, cleanouts, etc. Tubing or casing? Corrosion or scale?

B. Analytical—Field and Laboratory Tests:

Recommended Tests

1. *Water:*	Membrane Filter	Complete Analysis	Partial Analysis	Bacteria Tests
Supply water		x		x
Produced brine (sample all separate sources)		x		x
Composite water ahead of filters	x		*	x
Filtered injection water	x		*	x
Injection water at 1 or more inj. wells	x		*	x

* Tests such as iron, H_2S, turbidity, and dissolved oxygen are usually significant. The latter three should be made in the field. Production of H_2S downstream is cause for concern.

Appendix

2. *Deposits:* Note all possible conditions attendant to formation, occurrence relative to mixing of waters, aeration, etc. Samples should be sealed in jar and sent to lab before oxidation takes place. This applies to all samples of deposits, from any source. Any preventive measures used?
3. *Corrosion:* Record points of occurrence, frequency, any preventive treatment. It is most important that samples of corrosion be examined in the lab in unoxidized condition. Products of corrosion must be analyzed in order to understand the process of corrosion. Samples, such as pipe nipples, should be plugged with oily rags and sent to the lab without delay.

C. Interpretive:

In general, look for corrosion and scale in open systems. Similarly, fresh water, even from shallow wells, may cause corrosion due to oxygen when mixed with salt water. Such mixing can also cause scale. Microbiological troubles are generally worse with fresh water or when fresh water is added to brine. If both supply and produced waters are heavy brines, microbio troubles are usually minor.

Membrane filter tests serve to distinguish between good and bad quality injection waters. Color of deposit on the disc is indicative of air entry if brown. A black deposit means H_2S production and "black water" if H_2S is not indigenous to the source water. Absence of H_2S in water going to the filters but occurrence of small amounts below filter can mean only one thing—proliferation of corrosive bacteria in the filter bed and the need for filter bed inspection and probable treatment for bact. control. Anomalous occurrence of poorer membrane filter test below the filter than above has much the same interpretation. Where this rather common anomaly has been noted, tests showed the filter bed to be badly fouled with scale and organic growths

Appendix

so that it served only to innoculate the water stream with countless, harmful bacteria.

NOTE: The survey is changed, in view of existing conditions, with the objective of pinpointing the major troubles. It usually requires a minimum of 16 hr. total time.

Guide for Selection of Metals and Alloys for "Sour" Salt Water Service

Corrosion rates of insulated coupons 4½ x 1½ in. in SWD line, Darst Creek Field, Texas. 60 days exposure. Corrosion rates in mils per year (MPY) are averages of 4 coupons. Salt water tests: pH-7; H_2S-200 mg/l; Total solids–26,000 mg/l; temperature–120°F; Velocity–2 ft/sec.

Metal or Alloy	Corrosion rate, MPY
Nickel	1.0
K Monel	1.1
Nickel Plated Steel	2.8
Antimonial Admiralty	3.2
Type 316 18–8 (Mo)	5.5
Aluminum 6061-T6	6.9
Type 304 18–8	10.2
Type 347 18–8 (Cb)	10.8
70–30 Copper Nickel (70% Cu, 30% Ni)	14.0
Carbon Steel J-55	15.6*
Carbon Steel N-80	16.0*
Alclad	16.2
Croloy 2¼	17.8
Galvanized Steel	23.3
Croloy 5	23.4
9% Nickel	25.4
Copper Steel (0.26 Cu)	25.8
Yoloy (2 Ni, 1 Cu)	25.9
5% Nickel	27.3
12 Chrome Cast	28.7
3% Nickel	29.0
0.40 Carbon Cast	29.7
Croloy 9	30.1
Carbon Steel H-40	32.6*
Croloy 12	33.5

Appendix

Metal or Alloy	Corrosion rate, MPY
Corten (0.48 Ni, 1.04 Cr, 0.41 Cu)	35.6
Ampco Grade 8 (88 Cu, 10 Al, 1 Fe)	36.0
Cr-Mo-Si Steel (2.09 Cr, 0.56 Mo, 1.17 Si)	38.1
Everdur 1010	62.2
Copper Plated Steel	64.6
Red Brass Alloy 24 (85 Cu, 15 Zn)	67.1
Copper	107.8

* Common tubular goods composition

Reference: This work was done by Gulf Oil Corporation, R & D with Houston Prod. Dept., April, 1948.

It should be noted that the Alloy compositions and the conditions of exposure are not comprehensive. Thus, with the exception of a few metals and alloys of changeless performance, any indicated usage should be correlated in detail with all related corrosion data.

Appendix

Hypothetical Combination of Ions in a Water Solution

It is sometimes desirable to estimate the various salts which will precipitate from solution in a water upon concentration or change in temperature. These salts do not exist in solution. However, the chemical affinities of common positive and negative ions strongly indicate that a certain procedure should be followed in calculating the probable combination of ions.

The scheme most frequently used is described in "Standard Methods for the Examination of Water and Waste Water," 12th Ed., 1965, by American Public Health Association and the American Water Works Association. The following tabulation of compounds, or salts, in the order of ionic affinity, is based on the more complete discussion given in the foregoing reference.

Equivalents for Determining Hypothetical Combinations, in the Order in Which They React

$Ca(HCO_3)_2$	81.06	NH_4HCO_3	79.06
$CaCO_3$	50.05	$(NH_4)_2CO_3$	48.05
$Ca(OH)_2$	37.05	NH_4OH	35.05
$CaSO_4$	68.07	$(NH_4)_2SO_4$	66.07
$Ca(NO_3)_2$	82.05	NH_4NO_3	80.05
$CaCl_2$	55.50	NH_4Cl	53.50
$Mg(HCO_3)_2$	73.18	$NaHCO_3$	84.02
$MgCO_3$	42.17	Na_2CO_3	53.01
$Mg(OH)_2$	29.17	$NaOH$	40.01
$MgSO_4$	60.19	Na_2SO_4	71.03
$Mg(NO_3)_2$	74.17	$NaNO_3$	85.01
$MgCl_2$	47.62	$NaCl$	58.46
		Na_2SiO_3	61.03
$Ba(HCO_3)_2$	129.70		
$BaCO_3$	98.69	$KHCO_3$	100.12
$Ba(OH)_2$	85.69	K_2CO_3	69.11
$BaSO_4$	116.71	KOH	56.11
$Ba(NO_3)_2$	130.69	K_2SO_4	87.13
$BaCl_2$	104.14	KNO_3	101.11
		KCl	74.56

Appendix

The calculation of hypothetical combinations is made from the milliequivalents per liter, me/l, of the various ions determined in a water analysis. Multiply the me/l of the first anion listed (HCO_3) by the equivalent weight of calcium bicarbonate to obtain milligrams per liter of this compound. Deduct this me/l from that of the first cation listed (Ca), then calculate remaining me/l of the cation to the next anion, etc. In this manner the final remaining me/l of anion will exactly equal remaining me/l of cation and the sum of the milligrams per liter (mg/l) of salts thus calculated will be the same as the sum of mg/l in the ionic statement.

When appreciable silica is found in alkaline waters, it is considered to be present as sodium silicate. Usually, it is considered as a separate item. Iron and aluminum are usually considered separately, as colloidal oxides, although iron is sometimes present as the bicarbonate in fresh and brackish waters. Barium and strontium are frequently present in oil field brines and calculations by the above procedure indicate that these alkaline earths are present as chlorides.

Calcium Carbonate Equivalent Weight Factors

From "Boiler Feed and Boiler Water Softening" by H. K. Blanning and A. D. Rich, Nickerson and Collins Co., Chicago, 1935.

To change reported analysis in actual weights to weight expressed as calcium carbonate, multiply reported weight of each constituent by the following factors; to change from calcium carbonate to actual weight, divide by the factor.

Compound or Element	Chemical Formula	Factor
Aluminate	Al_2O_4	0.85
Bicarbonate	HCO_3	0.82
Calcium	Ca	2.50
Calcium bicarbonate	$Ca(HCO_3)_2$	0.62
Calcium chloride	$CaCl_2$	0.90
Calcium hydroxide	$Ca(OH)_2$	1.35
Calcium nitrate	$Ca(NO_3)_2$	0.61
Calcium oxide	CaO	1.79
Calcium phosphate	$Ca_3(PO_4)_2$	0.48
Calcium sulfate	$CaSO_4$	0.74
Carbonate	CO_3	1.67
Chloride	Cl	1.41
Hydrate	OH	2.94
Magnesium	Mg	4.12
Magnesium bicarbonate	$Mg(HCO_3)_2$	0.68
Magnesium carbonate	$MgCO_3$	1.19
Magnesium chloride	$MgCl_2$	1.05
Magnesium hydroxide	$Mg(OH)_2$	1.72
Magnesium nitrate	$Mg(NO_3)_2$	0.68
Magnesium oxide	MgO	2.48
Magnesium phosphate	$Mg_3(PO_4)_2$	0.57
Magnesium sulfate	$MgSO_4$	0.83
Nitrate	NO_3	0.80
Phosphate	PO_4	1.58
Sodium	Na	2.18
Sodium bicarbonate	$NaHCO_3$	0.59
Sodium carbonate	Na_2CO_3	0.94
Sodium chloride	$NaCl$	0.86
Sodium hydroxide	$NaOH$	1.25
Sodium nitrate	$NaNO_3$	0.59
Sodium oxide	Na_2O	1.61
Sodium phosphate	Na_3PO_4	0.91
Sodium sulfate	Na_2SO_4	0.70
Sulfate	SO_4	1.04
Sulfuric acid	H_2SO_4	1.02

Table of Conversion Factors and Equivalents

Given	Sought	Factor	Given	Sought	Factor
Ba	BaSO₄	1.70	Fe	FeS	1.574
BaSO₄	SO₄	0.4115	Fe₂O₃	Fe	0.6994
SO₄	BaSO₄	2.43	Fe	Fe₂O₃	1.43
SO₄	CaSO₄	1.417	Fe	Fe(OH)₃	1.914
SO₄	CaSO₄.2H₂O	1.792	FeS	Fe	0.635
Ca	Ca(HCO₃)₂	2.522	Na	NaHCO₃	3.654
Ca	CaCO₃	2.497	Na	Na₂CO₃	4.609
Ca	CaSO₄	3.397	Na	Na₂SO₄	6.176
Ca	CaSO₄.2H₂O	4.297	Na	NaCl	2.638
Ca	CaCl₂	2.77	HCO₃	NaHCO₃	3.65
HCO₃	CaCO₃	0.82	CO₃	Na₂CO₃	1.77
HCO₃	Ca(HCO₃)₂	2.657	SO₄	Na₂SO₄	1.48
HCO₃	CO₃	0.49	Cl	NaCl	1.648
CO₃	CaCO₃	1.67			
Ca(HCO₃)₂	CaCO₃	0.62		Miscellaneous	
CaCO₃	Ca	0.4004			
CaCO₃	HCO₃	1.22	Given	Sought	Factor
CaCO₃	CO₃	0.599			
			mg/l	lb/1,000 bbl	0.03504
Ca(OH)₂	CaCO₃	1.35	lb/1,000 bbl	ppm	2.857
CaO	CaCO₃	1.79	mg/sq cm	lbs/sq ft	.002048
CaCO₃	Mg	0.243	grains/gal	ppm	17.12
Mg	Mg(HCO₃)₂	6.018	ppm	Grains/gal	0.05835
Mg	MgCO₃	3.468	lb/1,000 gal.	ppm	120
Mg	MgSO₄	4.95			
Mg	MgCl₂	3.915			
Mg	CaCO₃	4.115			
Mg(HCO₃)₂	Mg	0.166			
MgCO₃	Mg	0.288			
MgSO₄	Mg	0.202			
MgCl₂	Mg	0.256			

Note: In the event that the above equivalents are found insufficient, the necessary factor may be derived as follows:

$$\frac{\text{Equivalent wt. of compound sought}}{\text{Equivalent wt. of compound given}} = \text{Factor}$$

For example,

$$\frac{CO_3}{2\,HCO_3}, \text{ or } \frac{60.011}{122.038} = 0.49; \text{ thus } HCO_3 \times 0.49 = CO_3$$

Specific Gravity vs Total Solids

(From Tech. Paper 432, Bur. Mines; A System of Analysis for Oil-Field Waters, by C. E. Reistle and E. C. Lane)

Sp. Gr. of Brine at 60°F	Approx. Total Solids, mg/l
1.020*	27,500
1.030	41,400
1.040	55,400
1.050	69,400
1.060	83,700
1.070	98,400
1.080	113,200
1.090	128,300
1.100	143,500
1.110	159,500
1.120	175,800
1.130	192,400
1.140	210,000

* The sp.gr. is not accurate below this range and thus does not give a good approximation of total solids.

With careful attention to cleanliness, calibration of specific gravity balance, temperature readings, etc., specific gravity may of course be determined accurately to 0.0001. However, due to time and necessary care involved, specific gravity is usually reported only to 0.001. Certainly, the quality of current water analysis data cannot justify sp.gr. determinations to 0.0001.

Appendix

An Editorial

Editorial from July, 1960 issue of "Corrosion," official publication of National Association of Corrosion Engineers.

HOPE SEEMS TO spring eternal in some people's breasts that the good genies will come up with a magical solution to their corrosion problems any day. This expectation that practical problems can be solved by recourse to the occult arts, or to some magical formula, apparently is the reason industry is afflicted with a constant stream of "gadgets," whose asserted functions are manifestly impossible under any known physical laws.

Most of these gadgets propose to control corrosion by water. This happens because it is easy to make a gadget of common, cheap materials, which will last when exposed to water at ambient or moderately hot temperatures. Also, because water is universally used and because its corrosion and scaling behavior is variable and difficult to predict without close technical study, it is a popular medium for the gadget makers to exploit.

Most of the gadgets profess to operate in one or more of the following ways:

1. A mysterious force changes the characteristics of a water stream so that the scale forming solids remain in suspension.
2. Magnetic force alters the water so that scale forming solids do not precipitate. Sometimes a claim is made that this force affects the ability of the water to corrode metals.
3. Electrical energy is applied to the water stream passing between electrodes powered either by a sacrificial anode or by an external source. Apparently direct current is favored over alternating, but this is not invariably the case.

Some of the super deluxe models may have both a sacrificial anode, a mysterious box or some other combination, the

Appendix

effect of which is said to prevent the water from being corrosive.

These devices have some common characteristics:

1. All of them are simple to install and require no maintenance.

2. There are no limitations on the volume of fluid that can be treated.

3. No adjustments and no supervision are required.

Generally, purveyors of these devices base their sales arguments on a stack of testimonial letters. Some of these testimonials if not all, are legitimate. Some of the men selling the gadgets apparently are not willfully misrepresenting the devices they sell, nor do they realize they don't work.

Those who buy the devices must equate testimonial with test to be convinced. Careful reading of testimonials often shows the claims of good results obtained are generalizations. No examples of failure are exposed. The assumption is that the gadgets are universally applicable and successful, no matter what the conditions.

Sales arguments are very carefully worded. This comes about because of actions that have been taken by the Federal Trade Commission against manufacturers who inadvertently made claims which could be measured against performance and were found wanting. Close reading of the sales arguments shows that claims are so general that it would be very hard indeed for the buyer to maintain later that specific measurable benefits are promised.

Sober reflection should cause any man, whether or not technically trained, to realize that the inferred benefits of these devices are wholly unrealistic (even if the theory of their operation is accepted) when weighed against the amount of energy that can be expected from the systems. In the case of some of the mysterious "boxes" whose function usually is stated in alchemic terms, there is no reason to expect any results, because no energy that can be measured is produced or even claimed to be produced.

Appendix

Don't be beguiled by a hypnotic spiel that promises you a solution of your corrosion problems without any effort or superivision. If it was that easy there would be no corrosion engineers and probably no corrosion.

API FORM 45-1

API WATER ANALYSIS REPORT FORM

Company		Sample No.	Date Sampled
Field	Legal Description	County or Parish	State
Lease or Unit	Well	Depth	Formation	Water, B/D
Type of Water (Produced, Supply, etc.)	Sampling Point		Sampled By

DISSOLVED SOLIDS

CATIONS	mg/l	me/l
Sodium, Na (calc.)		
Calcium, Ca		
Magnesium, Mg		
Barium, Ba		

ANIONS

Chloride, Cl		
Sulfate, SO_4		
Carbonate, CO_3		
Bicarbonate, HCO_3		

Total Dissolved Solids (calc.) _____

Iron, Fe (total) _____
Sulfide, as H_2S _____

OTHER PROPERTIES

pH
Specific Gravity, 60/60 F.
Resistivity (ohm-meters) _____ F.

WATER PATTERNS — me/l

STANDARD

LOGARITHMIC

REMARKS & RECOMMENDATIONS:

157

Generalized Design for Split Water Injection System

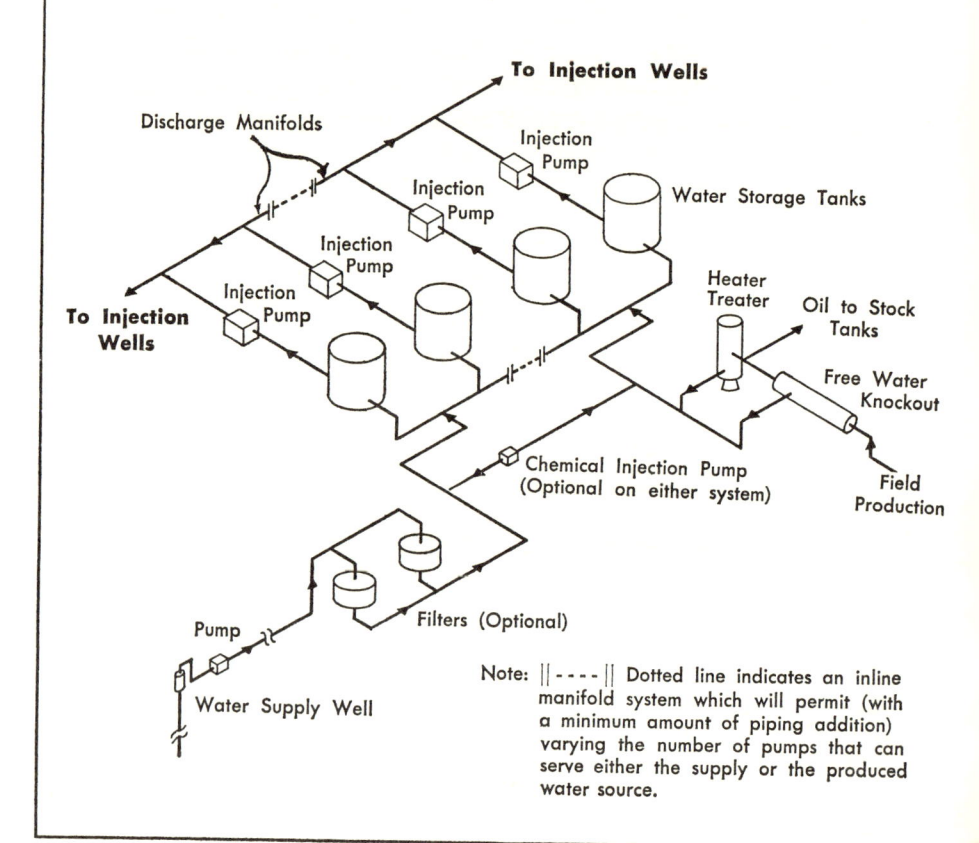

Note: ||----|| Dotted line indicates an inline manifold system which will permit (with a minimum amount of piping addition) varying the number of pumps that can serve either the supply or the produced water source.

General Index

The following index has been prepared for the purpose of providing a ready reference to specific problems due to water in oil production. The table of contents in the front of the book allows only general reference by chapter headings. Hopefully, this index will furnish an easy guide to descriptions of problems and their cure for field men using this book as an operating manual.

A

Acceleration of corrosion by dissolved oxygen, 46, 47, 20
Aeration cells, or oxygen concentration cells, 47, 48
Air flotation, effect of precipitated, colloidal sulfur and ferric iron on efficiency of, 140
Air leaks, damage from, 2
Algae and fungi, 53, 57
Algae – treatment with copper sulfate, 121
Anode – Cathode relationships, 48
Anaerobic bacteria and slime, 73

B

Bacteria and slime, 52
In filter beds, 59, 71, 92
Base exchange in clays, 92
Barium, incompatibility with sulfate waters, 13, 17, 64
Barium sulfate deposit, 62, 63
"Black alkali" soils, 104
Bimetallic corrosion, 47
Bimetallic gadgets, 108, 109, 110, 111
Black water, causes distinction between indigenous H_2S and that produced by bacteria 29, 30, 54
Black water in filters, 59
Black water plugging in injection wells, 119
Black water, treatment of, 120
Brackish waters and dilute brines, 13
Brines, absence of appreciable scaling and microbial growth, 5
Brine concentration and bacteria growth, 52
Brines, effects of oxygen and H_2S, 5
Brines produced with oil, 15, 16, 18

C

Calcium carbonate deposits, criteria for prediction, 34, 35
Prevention by polyphosphates, 68
Calcium carbonate, Method of recalculating to Ca and Mg, 10
Calcium carbonate stability index, 35, 36
Calulation of elements or compounds when reported as $CaCO_3$, 151
Calculation of gypsum solubility in brines by Metler and Ostroff Method, 33, 34
Chemical equivalent combining Weights, 7, 8
Chemical reactions in water, 6
Chemical reactions resulting in solid deposits, 24, 25

Index

Chloride pollution, 100, 101
Chloride values used in calculation of amounts of fresh and salt water, 103, 104
Chlorine – used for fresh water treatment, 119
Clay swelling, 91, 92
Closed systems, gas seals, 4
Coalesence of oil in oil/water emulsions, 129
Compatibility of waters indicated by "Palmer Values", 14
Complete water analyses and hypothetical combinations, 10, 11
Conversion factors and equivalents used in water analyses, 7, 8, 9, 10, 149
Corrosive bacteria and black water, 30
Corrosion by acid gases, 39. By oxygen and H_2S, 69
Corrosion by H_2S, 40, 41
Corrosion – field examples, 78, 79
Corrosion by sweet oil, or organic acids, 43
Corrosion – summary of conditions to avoid, 86

D

Demulsification procedure evaluation of oil/water treatment, 130, 131
Derivation of a balanced water analysis, 9, 21
Description of oxygen attack in salt water, 82. Prevention of, 83
Dispersed solids in injection water, 56
Dissolved air flotation for removal of suspended oil, 133, 134, 135, 136

E

Effect of dissolved oxygen, in presence of CO_2, on corrosion, 39, 40
Electrical gadgets, 107, 108, 109
"Electron Emitter" for water treatment, 113
Enrichment of waste water with oxygen by induced air flotation before disposal to streams, etc., 140

F

Field and lab tests at waterfloods, 144, 145
Field tests to identify deposits, 23
Field tests for water compatibility, 15
Filtration by diatomaceous earth, coal, 57
Flocculation and filtration, 121
Fresh waters, analyses of, 11, 12
Fresh water slime treatment with chlorine, 76, 77
Fouling deposits and organic matter, 51, 53

G

Galvanic corrosion, 47
Gas blanket, protecting power oil, 82
Graphitic corrosion by brackish water, 13, 18, 42, 48
"Gyp" water, 11, 17
Gypsum deposition due to incompatible waters, 64, 65
Gypsum solubility, influenced by chloride content, 26
Gypsum solubility curve, 27

H

Holding vessels – effect on deposits and growth of bacteria, 2
Hydrogen sulfide due to corrosive bacteria, 70
Hydrogen sulfide corrosion in absence of oxygen, 79, 80
Hydrolysis of organic salts in brines and effect on pH value, 34
Hypothetical combinations showing incompatibility, 67. Reference, 11

I

Incompatibility of waters, 13, 14, 15, 19, 73

Index

Induced air flotation ("Depurator") in separation of suspended oil, 136, 138. Examples, 139
Injection of unlike waters by split systems, 158
Injection water – general requirements, 85
Iron bacteria, 53
Iron compounds in water, effects of air and H_2S, 19
Iron sulfide accumulation, 68
Irrigation water specifications, 99, 100

L

Laboratory tests for determination of flotation cell size and chemicals for oil/water separation, 140
Limitations for salt in irrigation water, 99. For livestock, 100

M

Magic water treating devices, summary, 114
Magnetic iron oxide, due to oxygen in power oil, 81
Metals for "sour" salt water service, 147
Membrane filter tests, 88, 89, 91
Mixing waters, 2
Muck deposits, 72

O

Oil droplets in filter beds, 57, removal, 58
Oil in water "reversed emulsion", 123, 124
    Causes of, 124, stability and treatment, 125
    Napthenic acid, soaps and precipitated sulfates as emulsion stabilizers, 126, 127
Oil/water emulsion due to iron precipitation, 127. Increase of emulsion by scale treatment, corrosion inhibitors, acid-treating residues, microbio control chemicals, fire and steam floods, 128
Oil/water treatment by polyelectrolytes, 129
Oil/water treatment, examples, 132
Oil spillage, temporary nature of damage, 97
Open systems, 4
Organic matter in plugging deposits, 51, 52, 54, 74, 75
Organic matter other than oil, from membrane filter tests, 90
Oxygen corrosion, 46. Acceleration of pitting, 71
Oxygen corrosion due to air and brine in power oil, 81
Oxygen in brine, corrosion by, 4
Oxygen pitting attack, 81
Oxygen in flood water, effect on nearby "sour" producing wells, 93

P

"Palmer" values, calculation of in a balanced water analysis, 12, 21
Partial water analyses, field tests as guide to compatibility, 14, 15
Pitting attack, 87
Plugging deposits, 54, 55
Plugging material, sampling of, 29, 90
Pollution damage, necessity of early records and recognition, 96, 97
    By oil, 97
    By salt water, 98
    Calculation of damaged area by tests, 99
    Limits for irrigation water, 99, for livestock, 100
    Duration of pollution damage, 104
Polyphosphates for preventing scale in subsurface equipment, 31, 32
Prediction of gypsum deposits, 32, 33, 34
Prevention of solid deposits, 31

Index

Q
Qualifications for investigation of water troubles, 122

R
"Radioactive" gadget, 112
Reaction coefficients of radicles in natural waters, 8, 9
Removal of oil and solids by air flotation, 140, 141

S
Salt water changes by seepage through soil, 101, 102
Salt water primary production, salt water disposal and waterflood, 1
Sand filters, 73
Scales, appearance, tests, interpretation of causes, 23
Scales, description and tests, 25, 26, 28
Scale formation, due to mixing unlike waters, corrosion products, supersaturation, 22
Scale prevention by physical methods, 30
 In producing wells, 94
 Prevention in filter beds, 58
Scale removal, 30, 31
Sea water, compared to dilute brines, 13
Scaling, practical field tests, 87
Sequestering agents, preventing gypsum deposits, 66
Services, criteria for choosing, 115, 116
 Specifications, 117, 118
Slime deposits, organic matter other than oil, 74, 76
Slime formers, 85, 93
Sodium sulfate water, Permian red beds, 13, 18
Solid deposits, field example, 61
Solid matter in injection wells, 29
Specific gravity of water, relationship to dissolved salts, 10, 153
Sulfate reducing bacteria, 53, 57
Supersaturation, due to solution of reservoir rock constituents, 94
Supply water sources, 4
Surface water, effect of terrain, 102, 103
Strontium sulfate deposit, 62
"Stiff Index", 26, 65
Sweet oil corrosion, 49

T
Test nipples to detect scale, 26
Total hardness, calculation of, 12, 17
Treatment of insoluble deposits, 31
Treatment of slime accumulation, 74
Treatment of W/O and O/W emulsions, 129
Trouble finding at waterfloods, 144, 145
Tuberculation corrosion, 45, 46

U
Under scale corrosion, 45, 71
Under scale pitting, 119

V
"Versene" or "EDTA", action on acid-insoluble deposits, 31

W
Water analyses, balancing positive and negative reacting values, 9
Water analyses, hypothetical combination of ions, 149, 150
Water analyses, importance in treating O/W emulsions, 132
Water analysis report form, 157
Water chemistry, importance of, 2
Water compatibility, importance of, records 103
Water in oil emulsions, 123, 124
Water mixtures, designing against difficulties from, 3
Waterflood operating trouble, 5
 Planning against, 84
Water not suitable for fish, livestock and growing crops, 13, 17

Index

Well leaks, importance of water analyses, 142, 143
Well plugging by iron sulfide, 69, 70